Lisa Sanon-Jules

The Effects of Parental Level of Education

D1706395

Lisa Sanon-Jules

The Effects of Parental Level of Education

Social Capital among African-American College
Students

VDM Verlag Dr. Müller

Imprint

Bibliographic information by the German National Library: The German National Library lists this publication at the German National Bibliography; detailed bibliographic information is available on the Internet at http://dnb.d-nb.de.

Cover image: www.purestockx.com

Published 2008 Saarbrücken

Publisher:
VDM Verlag Dr. Müller Aktiengesellschaft & Co. KG , Dudweiler Landstr. 125 a, 66123 Saarbrücken, Germany,
Phone +49 681 9100-698, Fax +49 681 9100-988,
Email: info@vdm-verlag.de

Produced in Germany by:
Schaltungsdienst Lange o.H.G., Zehrensdorfer Str. 11, 12277 Berlin, Germany
Books on Demand GmbH, Gutenbergring 53, 22848 Norderstedt, Germany

Impressum

Bibliografische Information der Deutschen Nationalbibliothek: Die Deutsche Nationalbibliothek verzeichnet diese Publikation in der Deutschen Nationalbibliografie; detaillierte bibliografische Daten sind im Internet über http://dnb.d-nb.de abrufbar.

Coverbild: www.purestockx.com

Erscheinungsjahr: 2008
Erscheinungsort: Saarbrücken

Verlag: VDM Verlag Dr. Müller Aktiengesellschaft & Co. KG , Dudweiler Landstr. 125 a, D- 66123 Saarbrücken,
Telefon +49 681 9100-698, Telefax +49 681 9100-988,
Email: info@vdm-verlag.de

Herstellung in Deutschland:
Schaltungsdienst Lange o.H.G., Zehrensdorfer Str. 11, D-12277 Berlin
Books on Demand GmbH, Gutenbergring 53, D-22848 Norderstedt

ISBN: 978-3-8364-8882-2

TABLE OF CONTENTS

2

ACKNOWLEDGEMENTS

This dissertation is a culmination of many years of hope, faith and perseverance. What I have learned along the way is that success is never a solitary process. I stand on the shoulders of many and I am ready to take my place to help the next person. For this, I am extremely grateful.

First, my thanks go to God. Without obedience, faith and prayer I could not have made it here. To my husband, Emmanuel, you have shown an infinite amount of love, support and patience. I love you and I am grateful for all that you have done. To my son, Emmanuel (E-Man) for being so loving, patient and supportive while Mommy was doing her homework. Your unconditional love always sustains me.

To Dr. James Giarelli, I am so grateful for your guidance and vision. To Dr. John Young and Dr. Gregory Metz, I am thankful for your availability and support during this process. Dr. Eddie Manning, Milagros Arroyo and Dorene Pardun, your constant support and encouragement always kept me motivated and moving forward. I am also grateful for the support of Dr. Tanya Manning and Omorogiuwa "Uwa" Igiehon.

To my dad, your love and encouragement is the source of my strength. You have taught me the importance of hard work and education. But more than anything, from you I have learned about love. To my mom, you are a source of support and strength and I am extremely grateful for your love. To my sisters Gina and Chelsey, your love and support has gotten me through many tough times. I am very appreciative of your assistance in editing and proofing the numerous drafts that developed along the way. To Stacey, my Skooner, you are a constant source of strength and motivation. I can only say that you are the best. When God created you, he broke the mold.

" I don't think they play at all fairly," Alice began in a rather complaining tone, "and they all quarrel so dreadfully one ca'n't hear oneself speak-and they don't seem to have any rules in particular: at least if there are nobody attends to them…"

–Alice (Carroll, 2003)

CHAPTER 1
STATEMENT OF THE PROBLEM

Tinto's (1993) theory of individual departure identifies the lack of congruence between the student and the college as the root cause of attrition. The theory states that students from minority and/or disadvantaged backgrounds have a particularly difficult time adjusting to college (Tinto, 1993). According to recent data, the majority of disadvantaged students entering college will be first-generation students from blue collar backgrounds (Hsaio, 1992; Joseph, 1995; Noel, 1991). First-generation college students, defined by the US Department of Education as those whose parents have never enrolled in post-secondary education, are typically Hispanic or African American and tend to come from low-income backgrounds (Nuñez & Cuccaro-Alammis, 1998; Horn & Nuñez, 2000). The research indicates that first-generation and minority students face unique challenges becoming academically and socially integrated into college. Hence, it is important to investigate the effects of parental level of education on the experience of first-generation minority college students. This research will compare the experience of first and second-generation African American students in the first year of college.

First-Generation College Students

Studies of first-generation students have shown that they do not experience the academic success of second-generation college students (Horn & Nuñez, 2000; McConnell, 2000) and are at greater risk of attrition (Billson & Terry, 1982; Horn & Nuñez, 2000; Terenzini, Springer, Yeager, Pascarella & Nora, 1996), largely due to their inability to become academically and socially integrated into college (Billson & Terry, 1982; Terenzini et al., 1996). The difficulty that first-generation students face in becoming academically and socially integrated into the institution affects both their experience of, and rates of retention in, college (Terenzini et. al, 1996; Ting, 1998). Researchers have identified socioeconomic influences in the retention of first-generation students, including inadequate academic preparation, a perceived lack of family support, and differences in the perception of the college environment as compared to second-generation college students (Billson & Terry, 1982; Pascarella et al., 2004; Pascarella & Terenzini, 1991; Terenzini et al., 1996).

Despite these difficulties, first-generation students are a growing population. In 1995, first-generation students made up 45% of all undergraduates (ERI & IHEP, 1997). By the year 2000, 264,000 of the 1.3 million first-time freshmen who took the SAT were first-generation

5

students (Toppo, 2004). Unfortunately, once in college, studies have shown that first-generation students are more likely to drop-out during their first semester, attain lower grades and persist through graduation at lower rates than their peers (Inmann & Mayes, 1999; Riehl, 1994). Therefore, understanding the contextual factors that impact the college experience of first-generation students is important for college educators and administrators (Horn & Nuñez, 2000).

The Academic Experience of First-Generation and African American Students

Like African American students, first-generation students are considered to be 'at-risk' for retention in college. Heisserer & Parette (2002) define 'at-risk' students as those having academic disadvantage, low socioeconomic status or identification as a member of a minority group. Research on the postsecondary success of at-risk students finds that a student's academic preparation for college is highly related to their parent's level of education (Warburton, Bugarin & Nuñez, 2001). Students of parents who have not attended college tend to have lower high school grade point averages, lower SAT scores, fewer advanced placement courses and lower rates of graduation from high school than their peers (Riehl, 1994; Warburton et. al., 2001). The literature indicates that first-generation college students are less academically integrated than second-generation students (McConnell, 2000; Nuñez & Cuccaro-Alammis, 1998; Pascarella & Terenzini, 1991) and that their early academic experiences place them at a disadvantage once they get to college (ERI & IHEP, 1997). Once in college, poor students and students of color are less likely to finish college and are more likely to attend low prestige colleges or institutions with high drop-out rates (McDonough, 1997). Upon entering college, they display lower rates of math and writing proficiency and lack the level of critical thinking skills obtained by second-generation students (Terenzini, et al., 1996; Warburton et al., 2001).

The failure to become academically integrated into college has long-term effects for first-generation African American college students. While black students represent 11% of all students in higher education, they earn only 7.8% of all bachelor's degrees ("Business Remains", 2003). This is important since Black students tend to be more career oriented than their peers and shape their academic plans accordingly (Billson & Terry, 1982; Cheatham, 1990; "Business Remains", 2000; Helm et al., 1998; Pascarella et al., 2003; Schuman, 2005). The lack of academic integration for first-generation African American students is important because as the gap between minorities and non-minorities in higher education expands, there will eventually be

6

a large disparity in the types of career opportunities available to first-generation minority students (Lang, 1988).

Academic Integration: Effects of Parental Level of Education & Socioeconomic Status

Integration is defined by Pascarella and Terenzini (1991) as the degree to which a student adopts the institution's values and adheres to its formal and informal rules. Pascarella and Terenzini's 1991 study of college students showed that first-generation students experience lower levels of academic and social integration than students of college-educated parents.

The absence of college-educated parents contributes to the difficulties faced by first-generation students in integrating into both the academic and social aspects of college (McConnell, 2000), and in taking advantage of the personal and occupational benefits offered by a college education. Researchers have been aware that parental level of education, or the broader aspect of socioeconomic status, is positively related to student persistence (Terenzini et al., 1996; York-Anderson & Bowman, 1991). First-generation students do not have the benefit of college educated parents who understand the academic demands that they face or who are familiar with navigating the institutional bureaucracies of college. Blau & Duncan (1967) found that family income is highly correlated with occupation, which is largely determined by education (Billson & Terry, 1982). This indicates that the level of support that parents can offer their college students is related to the parent's level of education (Stage & Hossler, 1989). The influence of socioeconomic factors on parental level of support has implications on the academic, economic and career success of first-generation college students.

First-generation students indicate that their prime reason for attending college is for career preparation, as compared to second-generation students who seek personal growth through college (Billson & Terry, 1982; McConnell, 2000). The impetus for a focused career path is rooted within the family structure of first-generation students. Because of financial constraints, first-generation students tend to live at home during college and tend to work longer hours at off-campus jobs (Billson & Terry, 1982). First-generation students are expected to complete their degrees quickly so that they may financially assist siblings and other family members. Compounding the fiscal expectations of the family, the first-generation student must also consider the strain on resources that college places on the family. The additional pressure further hastens the student's desire to complete their degree quickly, which may negatively impact the student's academic and social integration into the college environment.

7

Researchers have hypothesized that children of college-educated parents are more aware of the demands of college (York-Anderson & Bowman, 1991) and that this impacts their integration into the college environment. Studies have indicated a gap in the understanding of college among families with lower levels of parental education. This gap is most evident in decisions regarding the choice of a college major. Parents of first-generation students may unintentionally hinder the academic and social integration of their students by offering erroneous advice about college courses and career alternatives (Inmann & Mayes, 1999).

Social Integration: Effects of Parental Level of Education on the Experience of the College Environment

The experience of 'student-institution fit' is an important factor in the process of academic and social integration because it significantly impacts the retention rates of students (Spady, 1970; Tinto, 1993). Social integration refers to the level of comfort that a student feels toward his or her college environment and its effect on student persistence. According to the literature on the experience of college, colleges represent a unique culture for first-generation students who experience a form of culture shock or border crossing (Inmann & Mayes, 1999; London, 1989; Terenzini et al., 1994). This experience causes first-generation students to feel isolated from the college environment and less socially accepted than their peers (McGreggor et al., 1991). These feelings of alienation can affect the student's level of involvement in the college.

Utilizing a composite index that measured contact with faculty outside of the classroom, frequency of meetings with academic advisers, regularity of going out with school friends, and level of participation in college organizations and activities, researchers at the National Center for Educational Statistics (1998) found that first-generation students are less socially integrated into the college environment than their peers. Similarly, Gibbons (2004) found that first-generation students are less likely to be involved in campus activities and other experiences which would connect them to the college.

One reason why first-generation college students are less socially integrated into the college environment is because they face conflicting obligations of school, work and family (Billson & Terry, 1982). Once in school, first-generation students are less likely to be involved in campus organizations and are more likely to have their most significant friendships with peers outside of the college (Billson & Terry, 1982). According to Tinto's (1993) work on retention, a

8

student's lack of integration into the college results in a lowered commitment to school and increases the probability that the student will fail to persist (Tinto, 1993).

To help bridge the gap in retention between first and second-generation students, state and federal programs like TRIO have been created to retain first-generation students through college. However, current retention efforts are restricted by stringent income guidelines and do not reach all first-generation students. The research indicates that the number of first-generation students attending college is increasing (Baker & Velez, 1996; Ishitani & DesJardins, 2002), particularly since the attainment of a college degree has become important for career mobility (Hsaio, 1992; London, 1992, p. 6). Although researchers have begun to compare the experiences of first and second-generation students (Billson & Terry, 1982; Pascarella et al., 2004), they have not addressed these differences within the African American community.

Quality of Effort

Previous studies of low-income minority students have focused on theories of educational achievement, status attainment and social capital, looking primarily at the elementary and secondary school levels (Anyon, 1997; Conchas, 2001; Noguera, 2003). The purpose of this research is to offer a different perspective on the impact of parental level of education on the educational experiences of African American students. This research will compare first and second-generation African American college students by focusing on the quality of effort invested by students in their own learning and development. The term quality of effort refers to the level of frequency by which students engage in activities that contribute to their learning and development. Pace (1979) observed that college outcomes are defined in large part by the quality of effort that students expend in maximizing their college experiences. A student's college experiences consist of activities not only from a student's academic program, but also from interactions outside of the classroom and efforts toward growth and learning. This investigation will explore the effects of social capital by studying how parental level of education impacts a student's quality of effort in, and experience of, college.

Quality of effort will be measured through examining the student's relationship with the college and its faculty and staff, examining how the students' experiences may affect their grades. This research will incorporate the theoretical framework provided by Putnam's (1995, 2000) work on social capital with the Tinto (1993) retention model to provide information for educators on how they can understand the effects of parental level of education on the quality of effort expended by African American students.

To compare the experiences of first and second-generation African American college students, this research will utilize the 4th edition of the College Student Experiences Questionnaire (CSEQ). The CSEQ, developed by C. Robert Pace in 1979, is designed to measure the quality of effort undergraduates invest in utilizing educational resources and opportunities for growth and learning. The CSEQ quantifies student perceptions of how well the campus environment emphasizes educational priorities, and how student efforts and perceptions relate to personal estimates of progress toward learning outcomes.

Purpose of the Study

Previous studies of low-income and minority students have focused on the gap in educational achievement between these students and their counterparts (Anyon, 1997; Conchas, 2001; Noguera, 2003). These studies have used status attainment or social capital models and focused on the elementary and secondary school levels. The purpose of this research is to offer a different perspective as it relates to the student's experience in college as measured by the parents' level of education. This research will compare first-year first and second-generation African American college students. The comparison will focus on the relationship between parental level of education and the quality of effort invested by students in their own learning and development, as measured by the College Student Experiences Questionnaire. This study will utilize the Tinto model (1993) of retention to provide educators with information on how parental level of education impacts a student's experience of, and integration with, the college environment. Since the literature specifically focusing on first-generation African American college students is sparse, the search strategy for this research will focus on literature concerning college students defined as being first-generation, African American, minority and/or low-income.

Research Questions

The purpose of this study is to compare the experience of first and second-generation African American college students by examining the following:

10

a) Is there a significant relationship between the perception of the college environment and the quality of student effort? b) Does parents' level of education have a significant relationship to students' perception of the college environment? c) Does parents' level of education have a significant relationship with students' perception of vocational and practical emphasis? d) Does students' quality of effort have a significant relationship to anticipated grade point average in the second semester of the first-year?

Terms

Terms used in this study that may require clarification are the following:

First-generation college students are defined in this study as students with neither parent having graduated from a four-year college (Ishitani, 2003; Joseph, 1995).

Second-generation college students are those with at least one parent who graduated from a four-year college.

Parental level of education is defined in this study as whether or not one or both parents have graduated from college, as indicated by the student's response on the CSEQ.

African American students in this study are those who self-identify as Black or African American.

Quality of effort describes the interaction between the student and the college environment (Gonyea et al., 2003) and refers to the extent to which a student utilizes institutional resources for their individual learning and development. Quality of effort is measured by the CSEQ on 13 scales.

Practical and vocational emphasis is a college environment rating score on the CSEQ. This scale measures the student's perception of the college's emphasis on developing an understanding and appreciation for diversity, developing information literacy skills, developing vocational and practical competence, and the college's emphasis on the personal relevance and practical values of courses.

CHAPTER 2

LITERATURE REVIEW

This research focuses on the first-year college experiences of first and second-generation African American students. Since the literature specifically regarding this population is sparse, the search strategy focused on literature concerning college students defined as being first-generation, second-generation, African American, minority and/or low-income. In order to address the needs of this population, clarification is necessary on several levels, the first of which is to adequately define a first-generation college student and to explain the historical background of African Americans in the American educational system.

History of African Americans in Education

The study of first-generation African American college students begins with the history of Africans in America. From the beginning of the slave trade, Blacks were imported into America and immediately stripped of their language, religion and culture. Slave owners, fearing insurrection, prohibited slaves from becoming literate. Those who learned to read and write risked beatings or amputations by their masters (Irons, 2002). Southern states and slave owners feared that education would encourage independent thought and would give slaves the tools they needed to escape from bondage, so laws were enacted to keep Blacks illiterate (Anderson, 2002; Irons, 2002; Rippa, 1984). Since the 16th Century, African Americans have faced challenges in securing an equitable education. The earliest documented challenge by African Americans to the educational system was the Roberts case. In 1849, 5-year old Sarah Roberts was prohibited from attending the local primary school because she was Black. Roberts' family filed suit based on an ordinance which stated that any child 'unlawfully excluded from the public schools could recover damages'. Although Roberts lost the case, this marked the beginning of an organized effort on the part of the African American community to end racially segregated schools (Irons, 2002). Throughout the 18th and 19th Century, attitudes toward the education of Blacks remained largely unchallenged. Education for African Americans consisted of racially segregated and substandard facilities stocked with out-of-date texts and limited supplies (Irons, 2002). This inequity was reflective of the value that society placed on African Americans, who encountered limited educational, social and occupational opportunities.

12

The inequities continued in America's institutions, including institutes of higher learning, where the subordination of blacks was justified on the grounds of their perceived intellectual inferiority (Anderson, 2002). Even the most progressive of Southern whites believed that education for blacks should not exceed the elementary level (Anderson, 2002; Irons, 2002). African Americans continued to encounter barriers to higher education through legal and state mandates in the South and institutionalized racism in the North (Irons, 2002). Although Oberlin College admitted a few black students in 1833, very few colleges followed and those that did found themselves quickly disbanded or demoted to junior college status by local government (Irons, 2002). The Supreme Court's landmark Brown vs. Board of Education decision in 1954 began to address educational inequality while the Civil Rights Movement enabled blacks to make slow gains in rectifying the effects of Jim Crow segregation. However, the cumulative effects of poverty and discrimination continue to affect African American students, as evidenced through the achievement gap that separates them from their Caucasian peers. On the elementary and secondary level, Haycock (2001) discussed the achievement gap that separates low income and minority youngsters from White students. According to Haycock (2001), the achievement gap has widened since 1988, particularly in the areas of mathematics and writing achievement. By the time of high school graduation, African Americans and Latinos have math and reading skills equivalent to those of white students in the 8th grade (Haycock, 2001), this gap only widens as students proceed through high school and into college.

The Achievement Gap: Its Legacy on Post-Secondary Education

The disparate rates of academic achievement result in a widening of the achievement gap for low-income and minority students at the post-secondary level. The cumulative effects of the achievement gap are especially important for first-generation college students who are more likely to stop-out or drop-out of college (Warburton, Bugarin & Nuñez, 2001). Educational policies, such as the No Child Left Behind Act (2002), have attempted to close the achievement gap (Cavanagh, 2004). However, we have yet to address the legacy of the achievement gap in the post-secondary opportunities and experiences of underprivileged students. Since many of the college and pre-college programs supporting first-generation students, such as the federal government's TRIO Program, focus on poor and urban school districts, it logically follows that the academic distress experienced on the secondary level becomes regenerated on the post-secondary level. In fact, data from the US Department of Education indicates that minority students are more likely to delay their entry into college and are less likely to receive a post-secondary education than their peers (Orfield, 1996; Warburton, Bugarin & Nuñez, 2001).

In a study of the effects of social class on educational opportunity, McDonough (1997) found that previous literature on school success ignored the societal and historical forces driving minority student success in educational institutions. McDonough's (1997) study found that the idea of attending college was heavily influenced by the prompting of high school guidance personnel. Her research suggests that social capital plays a significant role in access to higher education for minority students. The data reports that African American, Hispanic and Native American students are less likely to understand the link between higher education and their desired careers, less likely to be adequately prepared for college and more likely to attend college in non-traditional modes (Horn & Nuñez, 2000; Hsaio, 1992; Nuñez & Cuccaro-Alammis, 1998; Richardson & Skinner, 1992; Warburton et al., 2001). African American students also tend to have parents with lower incomes than their peers (Nettles, 1988). Since family income is associated with educational background, discrepancies in family income and early educational experiences eventually affect the college experience of disadvantaged and minority students (Irons, 2002). Given this, this research focuses on the first year of college, looking at how parental level of education affects the quality of effort expended by African American college students and how African American students experience the institutional environment of college.

College Experience of African American Students

Over the past decade, the number of African American undergraduates enrolled in higher education has increased by 32% (Nettles & Perna, 1997). However, African Americans continue to be underrepresented amongst both undergraduates (at 10%) and bachelor's degree recipients (7%), relative to their composition in the traditional college-age population (14.3%) (Nettles & Perna, 1997). Researchers studying the college experiences of African American students in Predominately White Institutions (PWI's) have found that African American students often encounter difficulty in becoming academically and socially integrated (Carter, 1999; Chavous, 2000; Chavous, 2002; Pascarella & Terenzini, 1991;). African American students in PWI's have reported feelings of normlessness and isolation, making the academic and social transition very difficult (Tinto, 1993). Research on the experiences of African American students typically utilizes demographic characteristics as independent variables (Chavous, 2000). African American students, on average, have parents with lower income levels, lower prestige positions,

14

and fewer years of education than White students' parents (Nettles, 1988). These variables are often used to explain the difficulties African American students face in adjusting to and persisting through college (Chavous, 2000).

Carter's (1999, 2001) research on degree aspirations illustrates the long-term effect of the achievement gap on the college experience of African American students. Carter studied the impact of family socioeconomic status on educational aspirations and how socioeconomic status affects the student's interaction with the collegiate environment. Carter's research utilized longitudinal data to identify indicators of the student's socioeconomic status, as well as characteristics of the institutional environment. Carter found that the amount of support from the college that students perceived was contingent upon the student's ability, race, and socioeconomic status. As Carter's research suggests, perception of the college environment affects the rate of persistence among Black collegians. Upon entering college, first-generation African American students encounter typical college transition issues compounded by the interactions of family background, socioeconomic status and race. As Terenzini et al. (1996) states,

> In both pre-college characteristics and their experiences during their first year
> in college, first-generation students differ in many educationally important ways
> from the students higher education has traditionally served. Because of these
> different characteristics and experiences, they are also a group at risk. They are
> a group clearly in need of greater research and administrative attention if they
> are to survive and succeed in college (Terenzini et al., 1996, p. 20).

The First-Generation College Student

The majority of researchers specifically define a first-generation student by socioeconomic status and ethnicity. Van T. Bui (2002) identified first-generation college students as ethnic minorities from a lower socioeconomic status, typically speaking a language other than English at home and scoring low on the SAT's. Other sources and authors defined a first-generation college student as an undergraduate whose parents had either no education beyond high school or who have never enrolled in post-secondary education (Nuñez & Cuccaro-Alammis, 1998; Warburton, Bugarin & Nuñez, 2001). Although the specific definition of a first-generation college student may differ, most studies are careful to separate first-generation students from students with at least one parent who has received some level of post-secondary education (Horn & Nuñez, 2000). This study will define first-generation college students as those with neither parent having graduated from a four-year college.

The level of education obtained by parents has been shown to influence the academic success of their offsprings (Billson & Terry, 1982). In a study of the post-secondary success of first-generation students, Warburton, Bugarin & Nuñez (2001) found a high correlation between a student's academic rigor in high school, their standardized test scores, and the probability of college enrollment.

Across the literature, there are several issues and challenges particular to first- generation college students. First-generation students are typically Black or Hispanic, (Van T. Bui, 2002; Horn & Nuñez, 2000), come from low income families (Horn & Nuñez, 2000; Nuñez & Cuccaro-Alammis, 1998), are more likely to attend rural or urban school districts largely consisting of underrepresented minority students (Warburton, Bugarin & Nuñez, 2001), and may have English as their second language (Warburton, Bugarin & Nuñez, 2001). In high school, first-generation students tend to score lower on the SAT and take fewer Advanced Placement courses (Astin & Osguera, 2004), both of which affect their chances of enrolling in, and persisting through, college.

Influence of Social Capital Theory on the Educational Experience

Previous research on the educational experience of minority and low-income college students has a foundation in the status attainment literature (Carter, 2001; Pascarella, et al., 2003). Status attainment is rooted in Weber's conceptualization of status groups. Weber believed that educational institutions could serve two contrasting purposes, either to increase the meritocratic selection of individuals for privileged positions or to maintain dominant group control over scarce resources (Arum & Beattie, 2000).

By the 1960's, two competing theories of status attainment emerged in the literature (Carter, 2001). The first theory was that educational aspirations and attainment were dependent upon socioeconomic status (i.e. Blau & Duncan, 1967). The second theory stated that a student's socioeconomic status affected the way he interacted with others, and in turn the way that others would interact with him (i.e. Sewell, Haller & Portes, 1969). Whereas the first view would attribute a student's lack of academic success to low ability or low motivation, the second view

16

looks at the context of the student's environment. Current research findings indicate that the inclusion of social psychological variables accounts for more variance in the status attainment model than the Blau and Duncan model (Sewell et al., 1969).

Status attainment theory was discussed by Bourdieu (1973) in the context of cultural and social capital. The idea of social capital was later introduced into the intellectual agenda in the 1980's by James Coleman (1988) to highlight the social context of education (Putnam, 2000). Social capital is a modern twist on the status attainment model. Social capital is composed of specific styles, tastes, dispositions and worldviews influenced by individual cultural and social origins (Bourdieu, 1986). According to Coleman (1988), what is important about social capital is the access to information it provides. Since the accrual of social capital is dependent upon both the extent of obligations held between two actors, and the trustworthiness of the social environment, social capital is essentially a reciprocal relationship. Coleman (1988) found social capital to have public good qualities. Public good qualities indicate that positive interpersonal relationships create strong social bonds which lead to closure in the community (Coleman, 1988). Coleman's (1988) approach views social capital as having positive ripple effects throughout the community and his work indicates that there are ways through which individuals can utilize social capital to transcend their stations in life. In fact, much of the literature on status attainment and social capital is grounded in the theoretical dichotomy of inclusion and exclusion.

Putman (2000) addressed the dichotomy of inclusion and exclusion in his distinction between bonding and bridging social capital. Bonding social capital is inward focused, reinforces in-group loyalty and homogeneity, and excludes outsiders. Bonding social capital is good for fostering specific reciprocity and mobilizing solidarity. Bridging social capital is outwardly focused and is inclusive of people across diverse social cleavages (Putnam, 2000). Bridging networks encourage the diffusion of information and help to establish linkages to external assets (Putnam, 2000). As an example of bonding social capital, Putnam (2000) discussed the bonds of a women's based church group or an ethnic fraternity. As an example of bridging social capital, he offered the example of a youth service group or the Civil Rights Movement.

While efforts to address the needs of minority and first-generation students have tended to focus on creating bonding social capital through efforts such as minority mentoring programs or federally based TRIO Programs, this research posits that both bonds and bridges are necessary to assist first and second-generation African American college students. As Putnam describes,

17

"Bonding and bridging are not 'either-or' categories into which social networks can be neatly divided, but 'more or less' dimensions along which we can compare different forms of social capital" (Putnam, 2000, p. 23).

Metz (1995) described the impact of social capital as the particular 'ethos' that groups form. In common terms, social capital is the ability to gain access to certain advantageous resources based on who you are and what your 'social value' is. An individual's social capital is created through the influence of his community, socioeconomic status and family background. In this study, advantageous resources for African American college students include support systems, personal networks and research opportunities. The attainment of social capital in the collegiate setting manifests through the student's ability to effectively 'code-switch', or adapt, to both dominant and non-dominant structures. Access to these resources and developmental opportunities determine a student's relative level of academic, social, economic and occupational success.

In institutional or college settings, dominant groups use social capital to establish norms and gain access to advantageous resources. According to Metz (1995), those with congruent social capital advance quickly through institutional barriers, while others are hindered by an environment which appears to be hostile. The influence of social capital explains the inequities in scholastic achievement among social classes (Bourdieu, 1977). This research takes the perspective that social capital also has an effect on the quality of effort that a student expends during college.

Social Capital and the Collegiate Community

Whether describing one's ability to move in and out of social systems or determining the possibility of one's future educational attainment, social capital deals with issues of community at its heart. Both Bourdieu's and Coleman's ideas on social capital are heavily influenced by the work of Emile Durkheim. Durkheim's (1951) study of suicide looked at the ways in which individual choice of departure revealed aspects of the community's collective culture. In his work, Durkheim identified four types of suicide- altruistic, anomic, fatalistic and egotistical. The final type of withdraw from community is egotistical suicide, which occurs when individuals are unable to become integrated into the established bonds of the community. This is the type of suicide that Tinto's (1993) work on college retention centers, "Egotistical suicide provides the analogue for our thinking about institutional departure from higher education. It does so not so much because voluntary leaving may be thought of as a form of educational suicide, but because it highlights the ways in which the social and intellectual communities that make up a college come to influence the willingness of students at that college" (Tinto, 1993, p. 104).

Social capital, as discussed by Bourdieu (1973), Coleman (1988), and Putnam (2000) centers around an understanding of community and social interactions. Horvat (2003) further explained how social capital influences the experience of the individual in the community. Horvat stated that individual attitudes and decisions are based on perceptions of the environment and institutional structure. In turn, individual outlooks and actions are derived from personal histories and from the influences of race and class. In the end, all of these factors shape, and are shaped by, structural events and practices (Horvat, 2003). This, according to Horvat, creates a "continuous dialectical reformulation of lived experience" (Horvat, 2003, p. 4). This study investigates how the lived experience of first-generation African American students compares to the lived experience of second-generation African American students during the first year of college.

Parents' Level of Education: The Influence on Students' Social Capital

Recently, scholars in the literature of education have begun to focus on the impact of parents' level of education on students' experience (Coleman, 1988; Coleman & Hoeffer, 2003; McDonough, 1997; Orfield, 1996; Stanton-Salazar, 1997). Researchers have found that the parents' level of education significantly influences the students' access to and rates of success in college (Hsiao, 1992; London, 1992, Terenzini et al. 1996). Current research shows that first-generation students experience more challenges in adjusting to college than second or third-generation students (Orozco, 1999). The literature in this area suggests that children of college educated parents are at an advantage in gaining the information, skills and networking experiences necessary to succeed in college. Students of parents who lack higher education do not have access to this information and may be less inclined or supported in the decision to attend college. In addition, these first-generation students will be less prepared to deal with the academic and social challenges of college. Researchers have investigated the impact of first-generation status on the educational experience through the lenses of cultural and social capital (Gonzalez, Stoner & Jovel, 2003; McDonough, 1997; Metz, 2004; Pascarella et. al., 2004; Richardson & Skinner, 1992; Saunders & Serna, 2004; Stage & Hossler, 1989; Stanton-Salazar, 1997; Zallaquett, 1999). Whereas, cultural capital refers to the level of familiarity one has with the dominant culture, social capital refers to the ease that one has in forming networking relationships.

Research examining the influence of social capital in education has been limited to the pre-school (York-Anderson & Bowman, 1991), elementary (Noguera, 2003) and high-school levels (McDonough, 1997; Stanton-Salazar, 1997). These studies typically focus on the role of cultural and social capital on minority student success in either the experience of school (Coleman et al., 1966; Stanton-Salazar, 1997) or in the decision to attend college (Gonzalez, Stoner & Jovel, 2003; Hurtado & Carter, 1997; Hurtado & Carter, 1997; McDonough, 1997; Perna, 2000; Saunders & Serna, 2004).

In a study of high school seniors, McDonough (1997) found that the level and quality of education available to a student was a function of the student's accrual of social and cultural capital. According to McDonough's (1997) research, students of the lowest socioeconomic status groups were less likely to attend college. Low income and minority students who did attend college, were less likely to persist even when ability and achievement were high. Stage & Hossler (1989) studied the relationship between family background characteristics, parental encouragement, and the post-secondary plans of 9th graders. They found that parents' level of education was significantly related to their expectations of higher education for their children. In addition, they discovered parental encouragement to be significantly related to the college plans of students.

Perhaps Perna's (2000) study is the best indicator of the interaction between race and the parent's level of education on their offspring. In a study of 11,933 students enrolled in four-year colleges, Perna (2000) noted the importance of considering social and cultural capital in examining college enrollment behaviors. Perna (2000) discovered that African American and Latino parents had overall lower levels of education than their White counterparts and that their children subsequently lacked adequate levels of social capital necessary to pursue academic goals. African American and Hispanic students required a greater degree of assistance from high school personnel with the applications, essays and financial aid paperwork necessary for college. Perna (2000) concluded that social and cultural capital are important components in the decision to enroll in college, "In fact, for African American and Hispanics, social and cultural capital is as important as economic ability" (Perna, 2000, p. 136).

First-generation status also has social and economic implications among college students. The first-generation student does not have the benefit of having a parent who has been through the college process or who understands the difficulties associated with attending college. Since first-generation students are the first in their families to attend college, their departure from the familiar represents a form of 'border crossing'. The cultural and social capital frameworks suggest that individuals with college educated parents have an advantage over first-generation students in understanding both the culture of higher education and the relationship between college education, personal development and socioeconomic achievement (Pascarella, Pierson, Wolniak & Terenzini, 2004). Compared to their peers, first-generation students are more likely to be at a disadvantage in choosing a college, deciding what kinds of academic and social choices to make in college, and in accessing and processing pertinent information on completing a degree (Pascarella, Pierson, Wolniak & Terenzini, 2004).

In a study of 107 African American, Hispanic and Native American students at 10 public institutions, Richardson & Skinner (1992) investigated how the parents' level of education influenced the college students' decision making processes. Richardson & Skinner (1992) concentrated on three dimensions of the college decision making process. They first measured the role that college attendance played on individual goals; this was termed opportunity orientation. Next they examined the level of preparation, or the development of expectations about college. Finally, they looked at modes of college entry, which referred to whether or not the parent's level of education affected the ability of the student to attend college. Richardson & Skinner (1992) found that parents' level of education significantly impacted all three dimensions. First-generation students were less likely to understand the link between college and their future occupational and personal goals, were less likely to have been adequately prepared for college, and were more likely to attend college in non-traditional modes. Most importantly, as it relates to the difference in experience between first and second-generation students, the Richardson & Skinner (1992) study found that students of college educated parents reported feeling more of a continuity in their educational experience which facilitated their social integration into the college environment.

Although the college enrollment patterns for first-generation and minority students have been studied in the literature, relatively little is known about their early college experiences (Pascarella et al., 2004). What the research does show is that the pattern of persistence in college differs among both first-generation (Billson & Terry, 1982; Inman & Mayes, 1999; Pascarella et al., 2003; Pascarella et al., 2004; York-Anderson & Bowman, 1991) and African American students (Carter, 1999; Coakley, 2003; Perna, 2000; Walker & Satterwhite, 2002), as compared to their counterparts.

The research indicates differing college enrollment patterns between first-generation students and those with one or more parents who have attended college. First-generation status is particularly important for African American students who are disproportionately affected by external factors such as race/ethnicity, income and financial aid (Warburton, Bugarin & Nuñez, 2001). The impact of external factors on first-generation African American students contributes to the fact that first-generation students are less likely to obtain a post-secondary degree than other students (Billson & Terry, 1982; Nuñez & Cuccaro-Alammis, 1998). Not only is first-generation status negatively associated with academic persistence, first-generation students are more likely to 'stop out' of college (Warburton et al., 2001).

The research is rich in outlining the difficulties faced by at-risk students in college (Billson & Terry, 1982; Carter, 2001; McDonough, 1997; Warburton et al., 2001). In a study of the effects of social class and high school guidance practices on student's perception of college opportunity, McDonough (1997) found that minority students and those from low socioeconomic status groups were less likely to attend and persist through college. To persist through college, first-generation students must develop new norms and behaviors. Not only is the first-generation college student entering territory unfamiliar to his family, first-generation students often receive little support and encouragement from their childhood peers (Nuñez & Cuccaro-Alammis, 1998).

The new behaviors that first-generation students must develop to succeed in college, typically conflict with the norms of their families and peers in the community of origin (Billson & Terry, 1982). Family and friends often do not understand the college experience or the academic demands faced by first-generation college students, who tend to perceive their families as less supportive than do second-generation students (Billson & Terry, 1982). Families of first-generation students usually expect the student to complete their degree quickly to return and financially assist siblings and other family members. The financial burden of college is an important consideration for poor and minority families because investment in education does not create reciprocal dividends among siblings like the sharing of books or toys (Steelman & Powell, 1989), so it is often difficult for poor families to justify the expense incurred by college.

Researchers studying the impact of the family on first-generation students found that educational attainment is influenced by the number of dependents in the family, as siblings deplete the amount of available educational resources (Roscigno & Ainsworth-Darnell, 1996; Steelman & Powell, 1989). The financial and emotional strain on the family also hastens the student's desire to complete their degree quickly, which may impact their level of commitment and integration into the college. First-generation students typically justify the expense of college by focusing on their future income potential. In a study comparing first and second-generation students, first-generation students indicated that their prime reason for attending college was for career preparation. In comparison, second- generation students indicated that their main motivation to attend college was for personal growth (Billson & Terry, 1982; McConnell, 2000).

Compounding the inability of the family to provide a wide range of emotional and financial support, the experience of the first-generation student is marked by feelings of alienation from their neighborhood friends who are not experiencing the college environment (Nuñez & Cuccaro-Alammis, 1998). Billson & Terry (1982) conducted a quantitative study of 701 students to look at the link between persistence in college and parents' level of education. Students were categorized by first and second-generation status and data were collected from the college persisters and leavers in each group. Persisters were more likely to report that their best friends were currently enrolled in college. Among both persisters and leavers, first-generation students were less likely to have their best friends in college and were more likely to have their best friends at work. Billson & Terry's (1982) research concluded that lack of family and peer support made it more likely that first-generation students would suffer from social isolation in the college environment.

Terenzini et al. (1996) conducted a quantitative study to investigate variables affecting the cognitive development of first-generation versus traditional students. Utilizing a sample of 5000 students from 23 institutions, the research studied the academic and social integration of first-generation students. Terenzini (1996) found that first-generation students did not integrate into college the same way as second-generation students. First-generation students reported feeling less academically prepared for college, indicated that the college environment was discriminatory and reported experiencing more non-academic demands than their traditional second-generation peers.

23

The Influence of the Parents' Level of Education on the Collegiate Experience

Billson & Terry's (1982) research at a private liberal arts and a commuter state college, noted the importance of perception of the college environment on the attrition rates of first-generation students. In studying the effects of generational differences on college attrition, Billson & Terry (1982) found that second-generation students expressed feeling a wider range of perceived support from their families, including emotional support and assistance with school related expenses. Billson & Terry (1982) also found that second-generation students were much less likely to suffer from social isolation and associated loneliness. Similarly, in a study of the level of college knowledge, family support, and reasons for attending college, York-Anderson & Bowman (1991) found significant differences in levels of emotional and financial support between students with college educated parents and those without. York-Anderson & Bowman's (1991) data indicates that parents who have graduated from college are more familiar with the experience of college and are thus better able to provide a wider range of support to their sons and daughters.

Unfortunately, much of the literature on the experience of first-generation students in higher education tends to focus on the community college (Brint & Karabel, 1989; Gonzalez et al., 2003; Hsiao, 1992; Inman & Mayes, 1999; McConnell, 2000; Padron, 1992; Rendon, 1995; Richardson & Skinner 1992; Weis, 1992), where an overwhelming number of first-generation college students choose to further their education (Rendon, 1995). The research indicates that first-generation students have histories of poor academic achievement and come from poor socioeconomic backgrounds (Rendon, 1995), which may explain why a preponderance of the literature focuses on community colleges. In a study of first-generation college students, Rendon (1995) found that attrition rates were highest in two-year colleges and among minority and low-income students. Rendon (1995) posed that there was a difference in the experiences of first-generation students, noting that many first-generation, minority and low-income students lack the cultural and social capital necessary to make full use of the college's academic and social learning communities. In another study of community colleges, Pascarella et al. (2003) found that first-generation students had lower total credit hours and grades than all other students. Furthermore, Terenzini et al. (1996) found that compared to their cohorts, first-generation students completed fewer credits during their first-year, took fewer arts and humanities courses, studied fewer hours per week, worked more hours per week and were less likely to perceive faculty as concerned about students and teaching. A follow-up study in 2004 examined the same issue through the lens of cultural and social capital. The study found that the academic and social integration of first-generation students differed from second-generation students based on the ways that they experienced college. For example, first-generation students were significantly less likely to live on campus during college and had greater work responsibilities (Pascarella et al., 2004). Terenzini et al. (1996) concluded that these factors likely lead to the tendency of first-generation students to participate in extracurricular activities, athletics and volunteer activities at lower rates than other students. The study also found that first-generation students had lower levels of out of the classroom-related experiences with peers (Pascarella et al., 2004).

Not only is it typical that first-generation students receive less financial and emotional support from their family members (Nuñez & Cuccaro-Alammis, 1998) and are less academically and socially integrated into college (Pascarella et al., 2004; Terenzini et al., 1996); the lower income levels of first-generation students make them more likely to seek higher paying off-campus employment opportunities (Nuñez & Cuccaro-Alammis, 1998). Lack of financial and emotional support from the home, coupled with off-campus employment, contributes to the decreased likelihood of academic and social integration into the college environment (Tinto, 1993). In this context, examining Rendon's (1995) finding that the two most important factors in the success of first-generation students is in making the transition to college and in making connections once enrolled in college, it is no wonder why first-generation students are less likely to obtain a post-secondary degree than other students (Nuñez & Cuccaro-Alammis, 1998).

This research contrasts the experiences of first and second-generation African American college students because of the unique challenges they face in becoming academically and socially integrated into college. First-generation students come from backgrounds associated with high risk factors for attrition, so the barriers they encounter in higher education are not only academic but also social. As Nuñez & Cuccaro-Alammis state, "For many of these 'first-generation' students, post-secondary education offers both opportunity and risk, as it represents a departure from family traditions" (Nuñez & Cuccaro-Alammis, 1998, p. 1).

25

Influence of the Environment on the College Experience: The Tinto Retention Model

The ability to create academic, social and political exchange is highly affected by the educational and occupational success of college students. The challenges that first-generation students face in matriculating from college have been addressed. Yet, it is equally important to look at the first-year academic experiences of first and second-generation African American college students and to explore how their perceptions may be impacted by the academic and social structure of the institution. The Tinto model of college retention provides such a framework.

Tinto (1993) proposed a model of retention that looked at the longitudinal process through which students integrate into the academic and social systems of the college. According to this model, college persistence is a process rather than a solitary event. Tinto's model (1993) investigates the root causes of student departure, while considering institutional factors that affect persistence. According to Tinto (1993), student departure typically occurs within the first two years of college and emanates from several root causes: intention, commitment, adjustment, difficulty, congruence, isolation, obligation and finances (Tinto, 1993). The model views the process of persistence as a three-stage interaction between the student and the institution. In the first stage of separation, students begin to distance themselves from memberships in past communities and to re-evaluate previous norms and patterns of behavior. In the second stage, transition, the student adapts to new norms and establishes membership in the intellectual and social life of the college. In the final stage of incorporation, the student discovers and adopts behaviors appropriate to the college and becomes integrated into the academic and social life of the institution.

Tinto's (1993) model accentuates the importance of student goals and commitments in the process of integrating into college. Tinto's model (1993) shows how pre-entry characteristics, i.e. skills/abilities, family background and prior schooling, influence individual student goals. The pre-entry characteristics that Tinto identifies refer to the accumulated social capital that the student enters the college with. The formal and informal experiences within the academic and social realms of the institution determine how successfully integrated into the college the student becomes. This affects the student's level of commitment to, and persistence in, the institution. Tinto (1993) points out that investigating student perceptions of the college environment is important because perceptions determine how likely it is that a student will integrate into the academic and social realms of the college,

> The mere occurrence of interactions between the individual and others
> within the institution need not ensure that integration occurs- that depends
> on the character of those interactions and the manner in which the
> individual comes to perceive them as rewarding. Thus the term membership
> may be taken as connoting the perception on the part of the individual of
> having become a competent member of an academic or social community
> within the college. Therefore, no study of the roots of student departure
> is complete without reference to student perception (Tinto, 1993, p. 136).

Tinto's model (1993) stresses the difficulties that students may face in becoming academically and socially integrated into the college through the work of Van Gennep (1960) and Emile Durkheim (1951).

Van Gennep's (1960) rites of passage illustrate how individuals progress through life, moving from membership in one group to another. The stages that individuals progress through are separation- the removal from past associations, transition- the process of learning new skills and patterns of interactions for inclusion in new groups, and incorporation- the acquiring of new patterns of interaction and establishing competency in new groups. In the transition stage, individuals are left in a state of uncertainty and normlessness. Tinto (1993) relates this stage to the experience of entering college students. Whereas students who are familiar with the expectations of college may find this adjustment exciting, first-generation African American students may feel isolated and lost. This feeling of disconnect may lead to voluntary or involuntary withdrawal (Tinto, 1993), or what Durkheim terms as 'suicide'.

Emile Durkheim's (1951) theory of suicide has been applied to the collegiate setting by theorists such as Spady (1970) and Tinto (1993). The interest in this theory arises from the belief that the study of suicide can provide insights on the characteristics of our society and its effect on individuals. Durkeim (1951) explains fatalistic suicide as the result of excessive normative control, evolving from "excessive regulation, that of person's with futures pitilessly blocked and passions violently choked by oppressive discipline" (Durkheim, 1951, p. 276). Fatalistic suicide is experienced by first-generation African American students who may be ill-prepared for the academic rigors of the institution. Egotistical suicide occurs when the student is unable to become socially or academically integrated into the college community,

> Colleges, unlike the communities Durkheim and Van Gennep had in mind,
> are rarely so homogeneous or monolithic in character. Rather than being
> made up of a single dominant community, the great majority of colleges
> are made up of several, if not many, communities or 'subcultures', each with
> its own characteristic set of values and norms. Though it is true that many
> colleges are marked by a dominant culture, one that sets the tone for the
> college generally, it is not always the case that students have to conform to
> that culture in order to persist. But it is true that they have to locate at least
> one community in which to find membership and the support membership provides
> (Tinto, 1993, p.105).

Applications of the Tinto Model on First-Generation & Minority Students

Tinto's (1993) retention model has been widely applied to the literature on college students (Christie & Dinham, 1991), first-generation students (Billson & Terry, 1982; Pascarella & Terenzini, 1991), and minority students (Elkins et al., 2000) to describe the process of academic integration into college. Billson & Terry (1982) found that first-generation students approached college with the same degree of normative congruence as second-generation students in terms of their expectations about college. However, first-generation students were less socially integrated into college than second-generation students. Additionally, first-generation students were found to have lower congruity between their values toward education and their parent's values, and were characterized by lower institutional commitment.

Other studies have found significant differences in the way that first-generation students acclimated to the Tinto model. In a study of 3,331 students utilizing data from the National Study of Student Learning (NSSL), Pascarella, Pierson, Wolniak & Terenzini (2004) found differences in both the academic and social aspects of the college experience by first and second-generation students. First-generation students were found to be handicapped in their experience of college. First-generation students were more likely to live off-campus, attend college part-time and have greater work responsibilities. First-generation students had lower levels of extracurricular involvement and had fewer non-academic interactions with peers. The findings of Pascarella et al. (2004) were consistent with the expectation that family cultural capital plays a significant role in the college experiences of students. Pascarella et al. (2004) concluded that the social capital that college students gain through extracurricular involvement, may be a useful mechanism by which first-generation students can acquire additional cultural capital to succeed academically and benefit cognitively. Pascarella, Wolniak, Pierson & Terenzini (2003) concluded that first-generation community college students were less integrated into the academic and social aspects of college because their college experiences and educational outcomes differed from their peers.

Influence of the Environment on Quality of Effort

According to Pace (1979), college outcomes are a result of the role of student effort expended. Although Pace (1984) stated that the main criteria for assessing student outcomes is the acquisition of knowledge and the development of intellectual skills, he also acknowledged that the personal and social development of students is important. Unfortunately, administrators and policy makers typically negate the self-reported experiences of students (Pace, 1984). Noting that student effort and involvement is positively linked to outcomes such as satisfaction with college and persistence (Astin, 1984), researchers have begun to re-evaluate the importance of self-reported gains through student assessments such as the College Student Experiences Questionnaire (CSEQ). As MacKay and Kuh (1994) proposed, more research into the relationship between student effort and educational benefits is needed. However, since most assessments and studies of college outcomes focus on Caucasian students (MacKay & Kuh, 1994), this research will allow educators to examine how institutional policies and practices can be modified to assist members of historically underrepresented groups succeed academically and socially.

In the literature, comparative research on quality of effort tends to focus on the experience of Caucasian and African American students. Research in this area has yielded differing results in explaining collegiate experiences by race, but maintains that perception of the college environment is very important in the experience of African American college students.

Cole (1999) utilized the CSEQ to measure the impact of faculty-student interactions on student quality of effort. Cole (1999) surveyed 1,282 Caucasian and African American students. Cole's (1999) findings suggest that the perception of the college environment by African American students is impacted by their interactions with faculty, who African American students perceived as less responsive and supportive than did their White peers. Cole (1999) also found

29

that positive interactions with faculty were especially important for first-generation African American college students. In a comparison of student efforts and educational gains between Caucasian and African American students at PWIs, MacKay and Kuh (1994) administered the CSEQ to 2,856 students. Regression analyses yielded mixed results on the influence of involvement on educational gains by race. The results suggested that when African American students at PWIs are encouraged to take advantage of institutional resources to further their personal learning and development, they can succeed at rates comparable to their Caucasian counterparts.

In a similar CSEQ study among African American and Caucasian students at community colleges, Swigart and Murrell (2001) examined quality of effort exhorted toward educational goals and students' perceptions of growth and development in non-academic domains. The survey population of 552 students was randomly selected and regression analyses suggested that the relationship between self-reported gains, demographic characteristics and quality of effort differed among African American and Caucasian students. African American students reported higher gains in social, personal and academic growth than did Caucasian students (Swigart & Murrell, 2001).

Finally, DeSousa & Kuh (1996) measured educational gains through quality of effort by comparing 1,200 Black students at PWIs and HBCUs. Findings illustrated that Black students gains at predominately white institutions were not as significantly influenced by academic related activities. DeSousa & Kuh (1996) concluded that quality of effort in HBCUs tended to be greater than quality of effort at PWIs, due to student perceptions of the academic environment.

Significance of the Research Study

When first-generation students do make it to college, they report feeling that they know less about the college environment and have to study harder (Van T. Bui, 2002). This research seeks to add to the existing body of literature, a quantitative-based exploration of the outcomes of the first-year experience for African American college students, and information on how the parental level of education may impact the quality of effort expended by African American college students. This research will impact retention efforts in higher education, by providing administrators and educators with the information necessary to assist first and second-generation African American college students.

CHAPTER 3

METHODOLOGY

Participants & Procedures

The sample utilized in this study was obtained directly from the national database of the College Student Experiences Questionnaire housed at The Indiana University Center for the Study of Post-Secondary Research in Bloomington. The data were gathered through the distribution of the College Student Experiences Questionnaire (CSEQ) by individual colleges and universities, and included 1160 records from a nationally representative sample of four-year predominately white institutions, both public and private. The sample analyzed in this study represents colleges and universities of five different Carnegie types. The data utilized were culled from surveys administered mid-way through the spring semester of the first year and were stratified to select students self-identifying as Black/African American and in their second semester. To obtain an adequate sample size, representative of both first and second-generation African American college students, the data used spanned 2001-2004.

The College Student Experiences Questionnaire

The College Student Experiences Questionnaire (CSEQ) was designed by C. Robert Pace and introduced as a multi-institutional tool in 1979. The CSEQ is currently in its 4th edition and is a 190-item instrument available in both electronic and paper form. Since 1979, the CSEQ has been administered to over 300,000 students attending over 400 colleges and universities, making it the third largest national database on college student experiences (Gonyea et al., 2003).

Normative data from the CSEQ is comprised of four types of institutions: doctoral granting universities, comprehensive colleges and universities, general liberal arts colleges, and selective liberal arts colleges. The CSEQ relies on self-reported student data. Relying on self-reported data in higher education is not unusual, as many outcomes such as those related to attitudes, values, social practices and practical competence, cannot be measured through achievement tests (Kuh, Pace, Vesper, 1997). The CSEQ is designed to provide several measurements including the quality of effort that undergraduate students invest in utilizing institutional resources and opportunities provided for learning and development, students' perceptions of the extent to which the campus environment emphasizes a diverse set of educational priorities, and the extent to which students' efforts and perceptions relate to personal estimates of progress made toward learning outcomes. The CSEQ includes a Quality of Effort

31

(QE) score, which describes the unique relationship between students and their campus environments (Gonyea et al., 2003). Quality of Effort has been linked to academic achievement, satisfaction and persistence and is widely regarded as a critical component of research in the area of student development (Gonyea et al., 2003).

Quality of Effort (QE) scores, according to Pace (1984) are highly reliable and have obvious content validity. Item statistics reveal that all items are positively skewed and items within each scale are positively correlated, suggesting that activities have been appropriately clustered to create a useful scale (Decoster, 1989). The CSEQ collects information about the student's experience with the college on several subscales: background information, college activities, and opinions about college, college environment, and estimate of gains (Pace & Kuh, 1998). The section on background information collects biographical student data such as age, major and parental level of education. The college activities section asks students to rate their level of involvement in areas such as course learning, experiences with faculty, campus facilities, student acquaintances, scientific and quantitative experiences, and clubs and organizations on a scale ranging from "never"=1 to "very often"=4. The opinions about college scale measures student feelings about college and whether or not they would choose to attend the same institution again. The college environment subscale measures student perceptions of the college's emphasis on the development of scholarly, academic and intellectual qualities; aesthetic, expressive and creative qualities; critical, evaluative, and analytical qualities; understanding of and appreciation of diversity; vocational and occupational competence; and the personal relevance and practical value of courses. The college environment subscale is measured on a scale from "weak"=1 to "strong"= 7. The estimate of gains section measures the extent to which students indicate that they have made progress in areas such as vocational training and understanding of other people, on a scale ranging from "very little"=1 to "very much"=4.

Not all subscales were used for this study. Utilized scales are as follows:

•Background Information: consists of eighteen items that relate to students' age, sex, satisfaction with college, initiative in taking advantage of opportunities offered by the college, and academic aspirations for life after college. This section also asks about parental level of education, "Did either of your parents graduate from college?" Students may elect to answer (a) no (b) yes, both parents (c) yes, father only (d) yes, mother only or (e) don't know. For the purposes of this study, first-generation students were defined as those students with neither parent having graduated from college. Second-generation students are those with one or both parents having graduated from college. Respondents who indicated that they were uncertain as to whether one or both parents had graduated were excluded.

•College Environment: The CSEQ concentrates on aspects of the college environment by assessing student perceptions of the psychological climate for learning on ten scales (Gonyea et al., 2003). The initial seven scales rate the extent to which the college emphasizes various aspects of student development including scholarly, intellectual and practical activities (Gonyea et al, 2003; DeCoster, 1989). The responses are marked on a seven point Likert scale from strongest (7) to weakest (1). The three remaining scales refer to relationships with other students, faculty and administrators. These are rated either positively or negatively on a seven point Likert scale.

•Quality of Effort: The CSEQ is based on a simple premise, the more effort that students expend in utilizing the resources of the institution, the more they benefit. Pace refers to the interaction between the student and the campus environment as quality of effort (Gonyea et al., 2003). Quality of effort is measured through self-reported responses on thirteen scales of the CSEQ: library experiences, computer and information technology, course learning, writing experiences, experiences with faculty, art, music and theater; campus facilities; clubs and organizations; personal experiences, student acquaintances; scientific and quantitative experiences; topics of conversation; and information in conversations. Students are asked how often they engage in each of the activities and respond on a four-point scale, "never," "occasionally," "often," or "very often". Each Quality of Effort Scale arranges activities in a hierarchy or Guttmann-like scale progressing from relatively simple to more complex levels of involvement and effort (Pike, 1999). Approximately 50 percent of the CSEQ questionnaire's content is devoted to the measurement of quality of effort (Decoster, 1989).

•Estimate of Gains: Students reflect on the progress they have made in achieving 25 commonly acknowledged objectives of higher education in five major categories; general education, personal/social development, science & technology, intellectual skills and vocational preparation. These items reflect a student's holistic development in areas such as understanding self and others, gaining the ability to think critically, and acquiring relevant career information. This section allows students to make value-added assessments on their college experience

(DeCoster, 1989). Responses are recorded on a four-point scale, "very much," "quite a bit," "some," and "very little".

Data Analysis

Preliminary analyses were performed to examine relationships between demographic and primary study variables. First, Pearson-Moment Product Correlations were computed to examine linear relationships among the study variables. Second, independent sample t-tests were performed to examine relationships between the means of the two study groups in relation to the variables of interest. Finally, composite grade point averages were computed based on student's expectations of earned grades.

Hypotheses

Upon a review of the literature, this researcher hypothesizes that:

A) There will be a positive and significant relationship between the perception of the college environment and the quality of student effort among both first and second-generation African American college students.

B) Second-generation status will be positively correlated with perception of the college environment and first-generation status will be negatively correlated with perception of the college environment.

C) Parents' level of education will be positively correlated with students' perception of vocational and practical competence

D) Quality of Effort will be positively correlated with anticipated grade point averages of first and second-generation African American college students. In addition, second-generation African American students will have higher grade expectations than first-generation students.

CHAPTER 4

RESULTS

The purpose of the study was to develop an understanding of the relationship between quality of effort and parental level of education among first and second-generation African American college students. The relationship between quality of effort and parental level of education was measured by the College Student Experiences Questionnaire (CSEQ). Data were collected from 1,160 first and second-generation African American students in four-year private and public institutions of higher learning. This chapter summarizes the statistical analyses performed to investigate the research questions presented in chapter three. Statistical analyses used include descriptive statistics, t-tests and Pearson Bi-variate Correlations.

The chapter begins with a description of the participants in the data set collected. Because this study focuses on examining differences between first and second-generation African American students, each analysis will include a description of differences in the perception of the college environment and in the quality of effort expended by both groups.

Participants

Demographics

The data gathered spanned four academic cohorts of students in the first year of college. Thirty and one-third (30.3) percent of the surveys originated in the 2001 collection, 41.3 percent from 2002, 15.7 percent from 2003 and 12.7 percent from 2004. The majority of the students sampled were traditionally aged college students, with 98.8 percent reporting their age to be under 23 years. Consistent with national college enrollment trends, most of the students (63.8 percent) were female.

The data included both first and second-generation African American college students (see Table 1), although the majority (57.2 percent) reported second-generation status with at least one parent being a college graduate. The percentage of students reporting that both parents had graduated from college was 29.8, 10.2 percent reported that only the father had graduated from college, and 17.2 percent reported that only the mother graduated from college. 40.3 percent indicated first-generation status, reporting that neither parent had graduated. Less than 3 percent of the students sampled were uncertain as to whether or not either parent graduated from college.

The majority of the students lived on-campus in the residence halls (91.8 percent). Students reporting working on-campus was 35.8 percent, with the majority of students (22.4 percent) working at an on-campus position only 1-10 hours per week. Only 13.5 percent reported working off-campus and less than four percent worked more than 20 hours per week at an off-campus position. However, of students who worked both on and off-campus, 19 percent indicated that working took at least some time away from their academic studies.

Overall, the data represented a diverse array of majors, 17.4 percent of respondents reported a major in the social sciences, 16.9 percent reported a major in business, 14.4 percent reported a major in pre-professional studies, and 13.9 percent indicated a major in the biological or life sciences. Very few students, 8.1 percent, reported being uncertain about their major (see Appendix A). Students in the sample reported achieving well academically, 27.3 percent expected to earn mostly B's, 28.5 percent expected to earn mostly B-/C+ grades, and 25.1 percent expected to earn grades in the A-/B+ range. In terms of future professional goals, 87.0 percent expect to pursue an advanced degree after college.

Residency & Parental Education

The total number of participants in this data set was 1,160. As reported in Table 1, 466 were first-generation college students and 661 were second-generation students. Students with missing responses, and those who indicated no knowledge of parental level of education, were omitted. In terms of gender (see Table 2), respondents were 63.8 percent female. Among the 463 first-generation students who recorded gender, 306 were female, 154 were male and 3 chose not to respond. Second-generation students were also largely female (n=420), as opposed to male (n=235). Two second-generation students chose not to respond to the question of gender. In terms of residency, 94.6 percent of second-generation students reported living on campus (n=625), as compared to 87.5 percent (n=407) of first-generation students (see Table 3).

The majority of both first-generation (30.5 percent) and second-generation students (26.8 percent) spent only 6-10 hours per week on out-of-the-classroom school work. However, a greater proportion of second-generation students (56.4 percent) spent more than 10 hours a week on school work than did first-generation students (53.9 percent).

36

Table 1

Number of Students in Sample by Generational Status

	Frequency	Percent
First-generation, neither parent graduated	466	40.3
Second-generation, both parents graduated	344	29.8
Second-generation, only father graduated	118	10.2
Second-generation, only mother graduated	199	17.2
Do not know	28	2.4
Total	1155	100.0
Missing	5	
Total	1160	

Table 2

Number of Students in Sample by Gender

	Total Sample		First-Generation		Second-Generation	
	Frequency	Percent	Frequency	Percent	Frequency	Percent
Male	412	35.7	154	33.3	235	35.8
Female	736	63.8	306	66.1	420	63.9
Missing	12	1.0	6	1.2	6	0.9
Total	1160	100	466	100	661	100

Table 3

Living Arrangements of Students in Sample by Generation Status

	Total Sample		First-Generation		Second-Generation	
	Frequency	Percentage	Frequency	Percentage	Frequency	Percentage
Dorm, other housing	1064	91.8	407	87.5	625	94.6
Residence, walking distance	29	2.5	16	3.4	13	2.0
Residence, driving distance	66	5.7	42	9.0	23	3.5
Missing	1	0	1	.2	0	0
Total	1160	100	466	100	661	100.0

Grade Expectations

The research indicates that first-generation college students are often at an academic disadvantage because they tend to live at home and work more hours at off campus jobs. In this study first-generation students reported slightly lower expectations of the grades they would earn in their first year of college. As illustrated in Table 4, a grade of A was expected by six percent of first-generation students (6%) and slightly less than seven percent (6.7%) of second-generation students. Slightly more than twenty-four percent (24.6%) of first-generation students expected to receive grades of mostly A- and B+, as opposed to 27.6 percent of second-generation students. First-generation students expecting to receive mostly B's were 25.4 percent as compared to 28.5 percent of second-generation students. The low B to high C range was expected by slightly less than thirty percent (29.7%) of first-generation students and 27.6 percent of second-generation students. Only 14.2 percent of first-generation and 9.6 percent of second-generation students expected to earn a grade of C or lower. Consistent with the literature, second-generation students in the study were more likely to live on campus, spent more hours on out of the classroom schoolwork, worked fewer hours per week at off-campus jobs, and expected higher grades than their first-generation peers. The research questions addressed in this study were designed to test whether these differences would affect the quality of effort expended and the perception of the college environment among first and second-generation African American students.

Table 4

Expected Grades of Students in Sample by Generation Status

Grade	Total		First-Generation		Second-Generation	
	Frequency	Percentage	Frequency	Percentage	Frequency	Percentage
A	75	11.5	28	6.0	44	6.7
A-, B+	300	28.7	114	24.6	181	27.6
B	314	27.3	118	25.4	187	28.5
B-,C+	331	26	138	29.7	181	27.6
C & lower	132	6.5	66	14.2	63	9.6
Total	1152	100	464	100.0	656	100
Missing	8		2		5	
Total	1160		466		661	

Test of Research Questions

Question 1: Is there a significant relationship between the perception of the college environment (PCE) and quality of student effort (QE)?

The hypothesis for question one predicted a positive correlation between Perception of the College Environment (PCE) and Quality of Student Effort (QE). Pearson Bi-Variate Correlations were calculated to examine the extent of the relationship between the ten perception of the college environment and thirteen quality of student effort scales.

Correlations between the PCE and QE scales among first-generation college students were small to moderate, ranging from -.03 to .31. Some aspects of perception of the college environment among first-generation students yielded higher correlations with the quality of effort scales, such as the student's perception of the college's emphasis on information literacy skills or their relationships with other students, staff and faculty members. Other environmental factors, such as the perception of the institution's emphasis on scholarship and diversity, yielded smaller associations with quality of effort. The weakest correlation ($r=-.03$, n.s.) among first-generation students was between the perception of the college's emphasis on diversity and the quality of effort students invested in utilizing computers and information technology. The strongest correlation ($r=.31$, $p<.01$) among first-generation students was found between the effort

41

expended in engaging in various topics of conversation (including discussions on current events and social justice as well as ethical, philosophical and economic issues), and the perception of the college environment as promoting the development of aesthetic, expressive and creative qualities. This suggests that the more evidence first-generation students see of the college supporting the expression and development of creative qualities, the more likely they are to engage in varied conversations with members of the college community (see Appendix B).

Among second-generation students, correlations ranged from -.01 to .29. Higher correlations existed on some QE and PCE scales among second-generation students than for first-generation students. Second-generation students equated more effort with their perception of their relationships with faculty, administrators and students, as well as with their perception of the college's emphasis on the practical value of courses. Lower quality of effort was associated with perception of the college's emphasis on scholarship and information literacy. The weakest correlation (r=-.01, n.s.) was between quality of effort invested in the arts, music and theater, and the perception of the college's emphasis on the development of information literacy skills. A strong correlation among second-generation students was between the perception of the college's emphasis on the development of aesthetic, expressive and creative qualities and the quality of effort students put forth toward utilizing library skills (r=.26, p<.01). In other words, when first-generation students perceived the college environment as emphasizing the expression of aesthetic, expressive and creative qualities, they put forth more effort to engage in conversation with others in the college environment. Second-generation students who perceived the college environment as emphasizing the expression of aesthetic, expressive and creative qualities, opted to invest more energy into academic pursuits (see Appendix C).

In comparing the relationship between the perception of the college environment and the quality of effort scales among first and second-generation African American students (see Table 5), the standard error was computed to determine significance at the p<.01 level. The results uncovered seven significant differences among first and second-generation students, four of which involved the Quality of Effort Library Scale. Significant differences were found between the quality of effort invested in the library and the perception of the college environment as emphasizing the development of aesthetic, expressive and creative qualities; the quality of effort invested in the library and the perception of the college environment as emphasizing the development of analytical skills; the quality of effort invested in the library and the perception of the college environment as emphasizing the fostering of diversity; the quality of effort invested in the library and the perception of the college environment as fostering an appreciation for the practicality of courses. Significant differences in the correlations between first and second-generation students also existed between the quality of effort invested in computers and information technology and the perception of the college environment as emphasizing diversity; the quality of effort invested in student acquaintances and the perception of the college environment as emphasizing diversity; and between the quality of effort invested in utilizing acquired information in conversations and the perception of the college environment's emphasis on the fostering of relationships among students, groups and activities.

The first significant difference in the two correlations (first versus second-generation), between the quality of effort invested in utilizing the library and the perception of the college environment as emphasizing the development of aesthetic and expressive qualities (the difference in r is -.17), indicates a relationship between how the student perceives the college's encouragement of creative expression among students and how effectively students utilize the library and its resources.

A significant difference was also discovered in the effort invested in library usage and the perception of environmental emphasis on diversity (the difference in r is .18). The frequency of library usage was dependent upon the college's focus on developing an understanding and appreciation of human diversity among students.

A third significant difference in correlation by generational status was discovered between the quality of effort invested in the experience of the library and the perception of the college environment as emphasizing the relevance and practical value of courses (the difference in r is .20). The more students perceived the college as emphasizing the relevance of courses, the greater the effect on the students' usage of the college library.

A significant difference in correlation was found in the effects of generational status on the quality of effort invested in library usage and the perception of the environment as emphasizing analytical and evaluative skills (the difference in r is .21), suggesting that the college's emphasis on the development of analytical skills impacts library usage among students.

Another significant difference in correlation between first and second-generation students was found between the amount of student involvement in utilizing computers and information technology and the perception of the college environment as emphasizing the development of diversity (the difference in r is -.19). The amount of student engagement in information technology was affected by the student's perception of the college as valuing and appreciating human diversity.

A fifth significant difference in correlation was found between the quality of effort invested in student acquaintances and the perception of the college environment as emphasizing an appreciation for human diversity (the difference in r is .17), suggesting that the more valued diversity appears to be at the college, the more students engage with their peers.

Finally, a significant difference in correlation by generational status was found to exist between the quality of effort invested in utilizing information in conversation and students' perception of the college environment as emphasizing the development of relationships with other students (the difference in r is .16). In other words, the more supportive the college appeared to be of peer relationships and student involvement, the more effort students took to incorporate the information they gained into various aspects of their academic and social life.

Table 5

Correlation Difference between Quality of Effort (QE) & Perception of the College Environment

Scales of First and Second-Generation Students

QE	Scholarship	Aesthetics	Analysis	Diversity	Info Literacy	Vocational Courses
Library	0.08	-0.17*	0.21*	0.18*	0.06	0.14
Computer/IT	-0.01	0.16	0.15	-0.19*	0.12	0.12
Course Lrng	-0.12	-0.00	0.02	0.11	-0.09	0.03
Writing Exp.	-0.07	-0.01	0.04	0.08	0.07	0.03
Exp. w/Fac.	0.05	0.10	-0.15	0.15	0.03	-0.01
Art/ Mus/The.	-0.07	0.06	0.02	0.05	0.10	0.09
Campus Fac.	0.09	0.13	0.16	0.12	0.08	0.09
Clubs	0.06	0.05	0.12	0.04	0.02	-0.01
Personal Exp.	-.11	0.04	0.07	0.07	-0.06	-0.01
Student Acq.	0.02	0.06	0.05	0.17*	-0.06	-0.02
Science/Quan.	0.10	0.07	0.12	0.05	0.07	0.03
Topics Conv.	-0.08	-0.08	0.01	0.00	-0.04	-0.03
Info Conv.	-0.12	-0.04	-0.04	-0.05	-0.14	-0.05

*p<.01

QE	Practical Courses	Rel. w/Stud.	Rel w/Admin	Rel w/Fac.
Library	0.20*	0.08	0.08	0.02
Computer/IT	0.12	0.02	-0.08	-0.01
Course Lrng	0.01	0.02	0.03	-0.05
Writing Exp.	0.03	-0.01	0.03	-0.06
Exp. w/Fac.	0.11	0.02	0.07	0.03
Art/ Mus/The.	-0.03	-0.09	0.09	-0.13
Campus Fac.	0.11	-0.03	0.03	0.01
Clubs	0.08	-0.03	-0.03	-0.03
Personal Exp.	0.04	-0.03	0.05	0.03
Student Acq.	0.07	0.03	0.03	0.02
Science/Quan.	0.08	-0.14	-0.07	-0.05
Topics Conv.	0.06	0.01	0.08	-0.02
Info Conv.	0.07	0.16*	0.15	0.08

*p<.01

Question Two: Does parent's level of education have a significant relationship to student's perception of the college environment?

Hypothesis two stated that second-generation status would be positively associated with perception of the college environment and that first-generation status would be negatively associated with perception of the college environment (see Tables 6 and 7). T-tests were performed on the ten scales measuring perception of the college environment and only two differences in means were found to be significant, perception of the college environment as emphasizing analytical skills and perception of the institution's emphasis on establishing peer relationships.

Student means differed by generational status in the perception of the college environment as promoting a psychological climate for learning that emphasizes being critical, evaluative and analytical. On this scale, second-generation students scored significantly higher (M=5.71, S.D. = 1.24) than first-generation students (M=5.53, S.D. = 1.29), (t=-2.34, p<.05).

The mean scores of first and second-generation African American students also differed significantly in the perception of the college as emphasizing peer relationships. Second-generation students scored higher in their perception of the environment as emphasizing the development of relationships with other students, groups and activities (M=5.59, S.D. = 1.32), (t=-2.30,p<.05) than first-generation students (M=5.39, S.D. =1.49), (t=-2.30,p<.05).

Perception of the college's emphasis on scholarship, diversity and the promotion of aesthetic qualities indicated no significant differences among first and second-generation African American students. Scales measuring the institution's emphasis on student development in the areas of information literacy, vocational competence, and personal relevance and practical value of courses, did not show any significant difference. Finally, first and second-generation students did not differ significantly in how strongly they perceived the college environment as promoting relationships with administrative personnel or faculty members.

Table 6

Perception of the College Environment (PCE) by Generational Status

PCE	First-Generation, N= 438	Second-Generation, N=626
Scholarship	5.93 (1.22)	6.04 (1.12)
Aesthetics	5.30 (1.39)	5.21 (1.37)
Analysis	5.53 (1.29)	5.71 (1.24)
Diversity	5.09 (1.72)	5.06 (1.64)
Info. Lit. Skills	5.71 (1.28)	5.67 (1.30)
Vocational Courses	4.99 (1.37)	5.07 (1.45)
Practical Courses	5.10 (1.48)	5.04 (1.40)
Relationships w/ Students	5.39 (1.49)	5.59 (1.32)
Relationships w/ Administrators	4.98 (1.50)	5.08 (1.45)
Relationships w/ Faculty	5.30 (1.40)	5.39 (1.29)

Note. Means (with standard deviations in parentheses)

Table 7

T-Test Results for Perception of the College Environment (PCE) Among Sample

PCE	T Value	Significance (1-Tailed)
Scholarship	-1.56	0.06
Aesthetics	1.00	0.16

Analysis	-2.34*	0.01
Diversity	0.22	0.42
Info. Lit. Skills	0.50	0.31
Vocational Courses	-0.97	0.17
Practical Courses	0.73	0.24
Relationships w/ Students	-2.30*	0.01
Relationships w/ Administrators	-1.16	0.13
Relationships w/ Faculty	-1.06	0.15

*p<.05

Question Three: Does parents' level of education have a significant relationship to students' perception of the college's practical and vocational emphasis?

Hypothesis three stated that parents' level of education would have an effect on students' perception of vocational and practical emphasis. The practical and vocational emphasis scale measures the student's perception of the college's emphasis on four environmental scales, developing an understanding and appreciation for diversity; developing information literacy skills; developing vocational and practical competence; and determining the college's focus on the personal relevance and practical values of courses (see Table 8).

T-tests were performed on the variables related to students' perception of the college's vocational and practical emphasis. These factors include the college's focus on having students develop an understanding and appreciation for human diversity, information literacy skills (i.e. using computers and other information resources), vocational and occupational skills, and on the personal relevance and practical value of courses. A test of differences in the perception of the college's vocational and practical emphasis by generation status indicated no significant differences (see Table 9).

Table 8

Means and Standard Deviations of Perception of Practical & Vocational Emphasis Scales

PCE	First-Generation, N=438	Second-Generation, N=624
Diversity	5.09 (1.72)	5.06 (1.64)
Information Literacy Skills	5.71 (1.28)	5.67 (1.30)
Vocational Courses	4.99 (1.37)	5.07 (1.45)
Practical Courses	5.10 (1.48)	5.04 (1.40)

Note. Means (with standard deviations in parentheses)

Table 9

T-Test Results of Perception (PCE) of Practical & Vocational Emphasis Scales by Generation Status

PCE	T Value	Significance (1-Tailed)
Diversity	0.22	0.42
Info. Lit. Skills	0.50	0.31
Vocational Courses	-0.97	0.17
Practical Courses	0.73	0.24

*$p<.05$

Question Four: Does student quality of effort have a significant relationship to anticipated grade point average in the second semester of the first year?

Hypothesis four stated that the quality of effort scales would be positively correlated to the anticipated grade point averages of both first and second-generation African American college students. Furthermore, it was expected that second-generation students would have higher grade expectations than first-generation students. To test this hypothesis, students' expected earned letter grades were first converted into numerical grade point averages. Secondly, the new existing variable was recoded and correlated with each of the ten quality of effort variables by generational status.

Among first-generation students there were three significant relationships. The first significant relationship was between quality of effort expended in participation in clubs and activities and the student's expected cumulative grade point average ($r=.17$, $p<.01$). The second significant relationship was between quality of effort put forth toward course learning and expected grade point average ($r=.15$, $p<.01$). The third significant relationship was between the quality of effort expended in the arts, music and theater and the expected grade point average. Although not significant, a negative relationship was discovered between the quality of effort expended in utilizing campus facilities among first-generation students and their expected grade point average ($r=-.02$, n.s.).

Among second-generation students, all correlations were positive and eight were significant. The first significant correlation was between the quality of effort expended in course learning and the expected grade point average of second-generation students ($r=.24$, $p<.01$). The second significant correlation was between the quality of effort invested in clubs and activities and expected cumulative grade point average ($r=.19$, $p<.01$). Significant relationships were also found between expected grade point average and quality of effort in writing experiences ($r=.13$, $p<.01$); expected grade point average and quality of effort in experiences with faculty ($r=.13$, $p<.01$); expected grade point average and quality of effort in arts, music and theater ($r=.17$, $p<.01$), expected grade point average and quality of effort in student acquaintances ($r=.11$, $p<.01$), expected grade point average and quality of effort in topics of conversation ($r=.14$, $p<.01$) and expected grade point average and information in conversations ($r=.12$, $p<.01$).

In comparing the differences in quality of effort and expected grade point average by generational status, it was determined that a significant difference in correlation at the $p<.01$

level would have to be greater than r=.16. In this study, no significant differences by generational status were noted. However, both first and second-generation African American students rated the quality of effort invested in course learning, involvement in clubs and activities and involvement in arts, music and theater as positively related to their grade expectations (see Table 10).

Table 10

Correlation of Grade Expectations by Generational Status

Quality of Effort	Second-Generation	First-Generation	Difference (Second-First)
Library	.09	.10	-.01
Computer/IT	.04	.01	.03
Course	.24*	.15*	.08
Writing	.13*	.03	.10
Faculty	.13*	.05	.08
Art, Music, Theater	.17*	.13*	.04
Campus Facilities	.05	-.02	.07
Clubs	.19*	.17*	.02
Personal Experiences	.03	.07	-.04
Student Acquaintances	.11*	.09	.03
Science & Quantitative	.08	.02	.06
Topics in Conversations	.14*	.09	.05

Information in Conversations	.12*	.10	.03

*p<.01

A T-test was performed on the variables related to parental level of education and anticipated cumulative grade point average. The results indicated that a significant difference existed in anticipated cumulative grade point average by generational status. The second-generation students in this study scored significantly higher (M=2.97, S.D.=.54) than first-generation students (M=2.89, S.D.= .57), (t=2.31, p<.05). This confirmed that the second-generation African American students in this study had higher grade expectations than their first-generation counterparts.

CHAPTER 5

DISCUSSION

Previous seminal research has focused on the impact of college on students (Astin, 1984; Flowers, 2004; Tinto, 1993). However fewer studies have focused on ethnic minority (Astin & Oseguera, 2004; Carter, 1999; Carter, 2001; Coakley, 2003; Hurtado et al., 1998; Hurtado et al., 1999; Lang, 1988; Stanton-Salazar, 1997) or first-generation students (Billson-Terry, 1982; Hsaio, 1992; Joseph 1995; Lang, 1988; London, 1992; McConnell, 2000; Middleton, 1997; Nuñez & Cuccarro-Alammis, 1998; Padron, 1992; Rendon, 1995; Terenzini et al., 1995). This gap in the literature has been cited by researchers such as Dennis et al. (2005), "Although ethnic minority students are more likely than other students to be the first in their family to attend college (Terenzini, Springer, Yeager, Pascarella & Nora, 1996; Zalaquett, 1999), most research has focused on first-generation college students as a group, without focusing specifically on those who are ethnic minorities" (p. 223). Recently, researchers have begun to examine the experiences of racial minorities (Carter, 1999; Carter, 2001; Coakley, 2003; Gonzalez et al., 2003; Mercillo, 2002; Mickey, 1988; Saunders & Serna, 2004; Somers et al., 2004) and to compare the experiences of first and second-generation students (Billson & Brooks-Terry, 1988; Middleton, 1997; Pascarella et al., 2003; Pascarella et al., 2004; Pike & Kuh, 2005; Pratt & Skaggs, 1989; Terenzini et al., 1996; Warburton et al., 2001; York-Anderson & Bowman, 1991; Zalaquett, 1999). This study was designed to elaborate upon the effects of generational status on the collegiate experience of African Americans.

The question addressed in the current study was whether or not the freshman year experience differed between first and second-generation African American students in predominately white four-year institutions. Previous research found that family background characteristics, such as parental level of education, influenced student behaviors related to college persistence (Billson & Terry, 1982; Pike & Kuh, 2005). For example, offspring of non-college educated parents are less likely to live or work on campus, tend to have their closest friendships off-campus, and are less likely to be involved in campus activities (Billson & Terry, 1982; Richardson & Skinner, 1992; Terenzini et al., 1994; Terenzini et al., 1996). The research questions in this study focused on how first and second-generation African American students' perception of the college climate was related to their self-reported quality of effort.

56

Quality of Effort & Perception of the College Environment

This research found that the majority of correlations between the thirteen quality of effort (QE) and the ten perception of the college environment (PCE) scales were positive. This indicates that the more favorably students perceived the college environment, the more likely they were to invest energy into activities associated with college success. This finding is consistent with previous studies which found that students expend more effort engaging with the institution when they perceive their relationship with the college and its constituents to be encouraging, friendly and helpful (Flowers, 2002; Hu & Kuh, 2003; Lang, 1988).

Unlike previous research on minority student perceptions of the college environment, the current study investigated the influence of parental level of education on the minority student experience in predominately white institutions. Prior studies on minority student perceptions (DeSousa & Kuh, 1996; Flowers, 2004; Gonyea & Kuh, 1996) focused solely on their experiences in predominately white institutions (PWIs) or compared the experience of minority students at PWIs to minority students at historically black colleges and universities (HBCUs). In these studies, researchers focused on the effects of the college environment on African American students and found that minority students experienced a more comfortable social environment and performed better academically at HBCUs than in PWIs, "Furthermore, for some African American students, the decision to participate in the college environment as well as the channels through which they choose to participate are related to their perceptions of how well they, as members of a minority group, fit into the environment" (Chavous, 2000, p. 97). DeSousa & Kuh (1996) established a link between perception of the college environment and quality of effort in HBCUs, where African American students were found to devote more effort to academic activities due to their increased level of comfort. Overall, the research comparing minorities at PWIs with minorities at HBCUs suggests that African American students tend to feel socially and culturally alienated in PWIs (Chavous, 2000; Chavous, 2002; Lang 1988). Chavous (2000) attributed the difficulty experienced by African American students in PWIs to diminished socioeconomic resources in the home. Other research suggested that HBCUs provide more social and psychological support, and a greater sense of community and satisfaction, resulting in an increased likelihood of persistence through matriculation (Allen, 1992; Pascarella et al., 1987). These previous studies established a relationship between the quality of effort expended by African American students and their attainment of educational goals, but they did not examine whether the quality of effort expended or the perception of the college environment differed based on parental level of education. The current study confirms that significant differences actually exist in the experiences and perceptions of first and second-generation African American college students in PWIs. In particular, differences were discovered in how each group experienced the college library and perceived their relationship with other students based on parental level of education.

Prior studies investigating the discrepancy in the overall adjustment and persistence of African American and White students attributed the difference in the college experience to demographic characteristics associated with parents of first-generation students, such as lower income, less prestigious occupations and fewer years of education (Chavous, 2000). Similarly, Billson & Terry (1982) also investigated demographic characteristics and concluded that family income was highly correlated with occupation, which in turn was determined largely by education. These studies show that fewer years of education among parents is related to lower family income, which adversely affects students' overall adjustment to, and persistence in, college. The current research advances the literature by establishing a link between generation status and the experience of first-year African Americans in PWIs, as based on their perception of the college environment and their expenditure of energy toward activities related to academic success. This research will inform educators as to how African American students are experiencing college and how this experience differs as a function of parental level of education. This information can be used to advance minority retention by assisting first-generation African Americans in becoming academically and socially integrated into the institution.

Previous research has found that students of college-educated parents are more likely to develop strong relationships with other students (Billson & Terry, 1982; Richardson & Skinner, 1992; and Terenzini et al. 1996), become involved in clubs and organizations (Billson & Terry, 1982; Richardson & Skinner, 1992; and Terenzini et al. 1996), and be more satisfied with the college environment (Terenzini et al., 1996). In contrast, first-generation college students are less engaged in the academic and social realms of the college, and "compared to second-generation students, they have less tacit knowledge of and fewer experiences with college campuses and related activities, behaviors, and role models. In addition, parents are unable to help much, even if they are so inclined as they, too, lack knowledge of, on in some instances may find off-putting, certain activities that could lead to greater levels of engagement" (Pike & Kuh, 2005, p. 290).

Given the existing research, one could surmise that college-educated parents would be better able to assist their children with navigating the collegiate environment and, as a result, that there would be substantial differences in the PCE and QE experienced by first and second-generation African American students. In particular, one might even anticipate that differences would be found on the scales measuring the students' perception of the college environment as emphasizing vocational skills, the students' perception of the practicality of their courses, and students' perception of their relationships with other students, staff and faculty members. However, the first and second-generation African American students in this study reported only seven significant differences in their experiences. These differences included the relationships between the quality of effort invested in computers and information technology and the perception of the college environment as emphasizing diversity; the quality of effort invested in student acquaintances and the perception of the college environment as emphasizing diversity; and between the quality of effort invested in utilizing acquired information in conversations and the perception of the college environment's emphasis on the fostering of relationships among students, groups and activities. However, the majority of significant differences between groups occurred on the library experiences scales. Significant differences were found between the quality of effort invested in the library and the perception of the college environment as emphasizing the development of aesthetic, expressive and creative qualities; the quality of effort invested in the library and the perception of the college environment as emphasizing the development of analytical skills; the quality of effort invested in the library and the perception of the college environment as emphasizing the fostering of diversity; and between the quality of effort invested in the library and the perception of the college environment as fostering an appreciation for the practicality of courses.

Quality of Effort & Library Experiences Scales

The impact of a student's exposure to the college library has been shown to be positively related to academic achievement (deJager, 2002; Wells, 1995), and some have even theorized that the use of the library contributes to minority student retention (Kelly, 1995; Jones & Quartey, 1993). In studying the impact of college resources, Mallinckrodt & Sedlacek (1987)

59

found that the use of the library positively impacted retention for African American students and they noted, "These findings highlight the importance of special programs emphasizing the value of the library, through academic departments as well as through student affairs units" (Mallinckrodt & Sedlacek, 1987, p. 9).

The current study uncovered four significant correlations among first and second-generation African American students on the QE library experiences scale. The first significant difference in correlation by generational status was found between students' perception of the college environment as emphasizing critical, evaluative and analytical skills and the quality of effort invested in utilizing the library. The second-generation students in this study reported a strong positive relationship between their perception of the college as emphasizing the development of analytical skills and in how much effort they placed in using the library and its resources. This finding is reflective of the change in the institutional environment from one of teaching to one of learning, whereby college students are expected to take responsibility for their own learning and development. This finding is supported by the recent increase in literature advocating the importance of student involvement in the collegiate library (Kuh & Gonyea, 2003; Schilling & Schilling, 1999; Whitmire, 1997; Whitmire, 1999; Whitmire, 2001b). Overall, the second-generation students in this study indicated a greater sense of comfort in their institution's academic environment and appeared to be better acclimated to the learning requirements of the institution, particularly in regards to the use of the library as an information resource. It may be that second-generation students are more comfortable with meeting the intellectual and academic demands of the college because they are more information literate. Information literacy is the ability of students to locate, retrieve, analyze and utilize information effectively (Whitmire, 2001). It is possible that the first-generation students in the study were not as aware of the institution's library resources or how to appropriately analyze and utilize them. Perhaps, prior college experiences provide the parents of second-generation students with a greater appreciation of the library. It is likely that college-educated parents expose their children to the library at an early age and that they are more likely to encourage their children to begin library research early in their education. It is also possible that the differences found could be a result of parents being better able to prepare second-generation African American students for college and for the level of work and library research they would be expected to do. As Kuh and Gonyea (2004) found in their study of academic libraries and student engagement, "the library

60

appears to be a positive learning environment for all students, especially members of historically underrepresented groups" (p. 11).

These findings may lend insight into how colleges and universities can assist in the creation of information literacy for first-generation students. For example, colleges and universities could increase the information literacy skills of first-year students through early exposure to the college library. First-year orientations and pre-college summer programs could begin by introducing students to the library and its staff, as well as explaining the inner workings of the college library.

Significant differences in correlations by generational status on the library experiences scale were also identified both on the institution's perceived emphasis on diversity, and in its emphasis in developing aesthetic, expressive and creative qualities. Second-generation students in this study reported high positive correlations in both areas. This indicates that second-generation students increased their use of the college library when the institution appeared to foster an appreciation for human diversity and when the institution appeared to openly encourage the development of expressive and creative qualities among its students. A possible reason may be that first-generation students are more apt to experience psychological barriers to library usage. Whitmire (1997) reported that psychological barriers, such as stereotype threat, may account for reluctance among African American students in approaching reference librarians or in using library technology. In the context of this study, the phenomena of stereotype threat could explain how perception can negatively affect the sense of belonging, level of commitment, and academic performance of African American students (Spencer et al., 2004; Steele, 1997; Steele, 1999). Whitmire (2001b) found that requesting help from a librarian was the only library experience shown to decline over the course of a student's college career. Whitmire (2001b) suggested that the decline may be indicative of stereotype threat. This may be because African American students are afraid to ask librarians for help for fear of appearing incompetent. The research indicates that when African American students experience the college environment as accepting, and when that environment encourages open expression, they are more likely to experience a sense of belonging and to effectively utilize the institution's resources (Carter, 1999; Carter, 2001; Chavous, 2000; Spencer et al., 2004; Stamps, 1988).

It is likely that second-generation students, who have the benefit of at least one parent who has undergone similar undergraduate experiences, may not be as prone to stereotype threat.

61

It is possible that early exposure to the library by their parents has made second-generation students more comfortable in library environments. It is also possible that the parents of second-generation students have provided them with the skills necessary to confidently approach college and library administrators.

Combating the influence of stereotype threat would require aggressive action on behalf of campus libraries. Libraries would need to recruit and train staff of color and to provide diversity training for its non-minority staff. Ibarra's (2005) work on college libraries suggests instituting diversity initiatives focused on bringing students of diverse backgrounds into inclusive academic space. This means that students would experience the library as an environment open to positive views of gender, ethnicity and racialized issues. Creating inclusive academic space involves diversifying librarians, administrations and staff, as well as diversifying collections, resources and ways of providing services. To create a comfortable and inclusive environment for first-generation African American students, library staff can create programming targeted toward minority student issues. Libraries can also show their openness to diversity by creating environments with art work and literary collections that reflect the minority experience.

The last significant difference among the correlations on the library experiences scale involved the perception of the college environment as emphasizing the relevance and practical value of courses. In the current study, second-generation students reported a positive correlation between their perceptions of the practical value of their courses and their increased investment of effort in utilizing the resources of the library. First-generation students did not appear to find as much practical value in their courses and, subsequently used the library less. One plausible explanation can be found in the research on first-generation students and their career aspirations. Researchers have found that first-generation students place a high value on what they perceive as practicality in their academic and career choices. The baccalaureate degree is seen as an important avenue of social mobility and represents the ability to reap economic benefits (Kaplan, 1980; Pascarella & Terenzini, 1991), therefore families of first-generation students may be more likely to urge them toward majors and courses that appear to be financially sound. Since the first-year courses that first-generation students take are unlikely to move them toward their anticipated career goals, they are probably less likely to invest additional effort into these courses because they are not seen as directly linked to viable economic outcomes.

Another possible explanation for the difference in perception of the environment as emphasizing the practical value of courses is the socialization of second-generation students. The experience of college-educated parents may prepare them to better communicate the value of required courses and their relation to career and academic goals to their children. Karunanyalse & Nauta (2004) found that college students look to same race role models for information on how to challenge stereotypes and negotiate career tasks. It is possible that college-educated parents may fill this role for African American students. Parents new to the college experience may not see the practical value in some of the liberal arts courses and majors. In such cases, an overemphasis on the economic benefits of education may occur, outweighing the opportunity for personal growth and development.

The lack of a strong connection between library usage and the perceived practicality of courses for first-generation students indicates that they may be more focused on the vocational benefits of college. Relying on a college education for only vocational aspirations may have detrimental results for first-generation students. A college education provides a multitude of growth opportunities. Students who are focused only on the technical value of their courses are likely to miss out on the other skills that higher education endeavors to cultivate, particularly in the areas of networking and civic involvement. To assist students in seeing the practical value in all their courses, colleges must clearly delineate the objectives of their courses. Student affairs areas can work actively to translate the undergraduate classroom experience into viable civic and networking opportunities that facilitate mentoring and internship opportunities. In addition, faculty members must cultivate meaningful library experiences into their courses to showcase the relevance of the course to the students' lives.

QE Student Acquaintances & PCE Appreciation for Human Diversity

Another significant difference between first and second-generation students was found between the quality of effort invested in student acquaintances and the perception of the college environment as emphasizing an appreciation for human diversity. The second-generation students in this study reported a high positive correlation between their perception of the college environment as emphasizing an understanding and appreciation of human diversity, and the frequency in which they attempted to acquaint themselves with students whose backgrounds, philosophies or religious affiliations differed from their own. When second-generation students believed that their college encouraged diversity, they made a greater effort to connect with other students. First-generation students were less likely to reach out to other students, even when the college encouraged diversity. The research indicates that first-generation students are typically minority students, tend to come from low-income environments and tend to have weaker academic preparation in predominately minority schools (Dennis et al., 2005; Lohfink & Paulsen, 2005; Pike & Kuh, 2005; Pascarella et al., 2004 & Zalaquett, 1999). It may be that the prior educational and social experiences of first-generation students may not have adequately prepared them with the networking skills necessary in a PWI. Researchers define the ability to access and utilize human and physical resources, including people, as social capital. It is imperative that colleges make attempts to strengthen the social capital of all students. It is particularly important that the college take an active role in assisting first-generation students in becoming academically and socially integrated into college. The research clearly indicates that peer interactions lead to social integration, which has been shown to positively impact the rates of retention for minority students. Colleges can assist first-generation students in building social capital, and in becoming academically and socially integrated into the institution, through mentoring and summer bridge programs.

QE Information in Conversations & PCE Establishing Relationships with Other Students,
Student Groups and Activities

A related significant difference was noted by generational status between the quality of effort invested in presenting information in conversations and the students' perception of the environmental emphasis on establishing relationships with other students, groups and activities. Second-generation students reported a higher positive correlation between their perception of the college as emphasizing relationships with other students, groups and activities and the amount of effort they invested in engaging in varied topics of conversation. Again, this difference may be reflective of the difficulties first-generation students face in becoming academically and socially integrated into college. If first-generation African American students do not perceive the college environment as one where they fit, they are unlikely to engage in discussions about academic or social issues with their counterparts outside of the classroom.

The research shows that first-generation students face difficulty in becoming academically and socially integrated into the college environment (Billson & Terry, 1982; Lohfink & Paulsen, 2005; Pascarella et al., 2004; Saunders & Serna, 2004). This particular scale shows the relationship between the aspects of both the academic (presenting information in conversations) and social (relationships with other students) realms of the college experience. Colleges can assist first-generation students in becoming acclimated to the academic and social demands of college by encouraging collaborative group class activities, like class debates and group projects. Colleges could also incorporate the use of campus forums or town hall meetings into the culture of the institution as a medium for student expression.

QE Utilizing Computer and Information Technology & PCE Fostering Diversity

Finally, a significant difference was noted by generational status between the quality of effort invested in utilizing computer and information technology and the perception of the college environment as fostering diversity. Second-generation students in this study reported investing more effort into utilizing computers and technology when they perceived the environment as emphasizing diversity. The computers and information technology scale includes items such as communicating with instructors and students through e-mail, developing multimedia presentations, analyzing statistical data and participating in electronic class discussions. First-generation students in this study did not report a high correlation in this area, possibly because first-generation students come to college with background characteristics that put them at a disadvantage (Orbe, 2004; Terenzini et al., 1996). The research of both Terenzini et al. (1996) and Orbe (2004) allude to differences in the way that first-generation students utilize the institution's human and physical resources, and how they perceive their role within the academic and social structures of the college. Students of college educated parents are more likely to come from home environments with greater access to resources like computers. It is likely that the parents of second-generation students also emphasize the value of networking with classmates and faculty. The findings of this current research indicate that colleges and universities must make careful and deliberate efforts to incorporate technology into the classroom. It is important that instructors take appropriate time to educate students on the proper utilization of technology and that the instructors ensure that technology is readily available from the institution.

The seven significant differences in correlations by generational status found in this study reiterate that there are important differences in how first and second-generation African Americans perceive the college environment. These differences clearly indicate that first and second-generation African American students experience the college environment in vastly different ways in the first year of college, especially as it pertains to library usage and interactions with other students.

Generational Status & PCE

The current study found significant differences by generational status on two of the ten perception of the college environment scales. In comparing first and second-generation students, the first significant difference was discovered in how each group assessed the college's encouragement of developing relationships with other students, groups and activities. Consistent with the results of previous studies, the second-generation students in this study reported a greater emphasis on establishing relationships with other students than first-generation students. A possible explanation for this may be that first-generation students have greater work responsibilities, limiting the amount of time available for extracurricular activities and peer interactions (Pascarella et al., 2004). Supporting research found that first-generation students work significantly more hours per week, complete fewer credit hours, and have lower levels of extracurricular involvement (Pascarella et al., 2004). The additional responsibilities of first-generation students make it difficult for them to leave the social networks of their communities of origin behind to enter into the academic and social realms of the college.

Terenzini et al. (1996) found that first-generation students differed in their instructional, curricular and extracurricular experiences and perceived their college experiences differently. Orbe (2004) noted that first-generation students typically do not participate in student organizations or interact with other students or faculty. These findings indicate the importance of creating programming targeted to first-generation students. Outreach to first-generation students must include activities focused on assisting them in becoming academically and socially integrated into the institution. Colleges can create programs and activities that meet the needs and interests of their first-generation students and should endeavor to offer space and programming during non-traditional hours.

Second-generation students in this study reported a greater emphasis in their perception of the college environment as emphasizing analytical, critical and evaluative skills than first-generation students. One reason for this could be that college-educated parents may better understand and communicate to their offspring the overall relevance of a college education in developing life skills. Research by Billson & Terry (1982) supports this assertion. Billson &

Terry (1982) found that second-generation students perceived their parents as more emotionally supportive and willing to assist with school related tasks, such as homework. In that study, only 61% of all first-generation students found their parents to be emotionally supportive, compared to 73% of second-generation students (Billson & Terry, 1982). York-Anderson & Bowman (1991) found that previous research revealed important differences in the support structures surrounding first and second-generation college students and concluded that having a basic knowledge of the academic policies by which colleges operate provided a valuable foundation for first-year students, "This basic knowledge can be derived from a number of sources, including parents with previous college experience" (p.18). This current research shows that the support structure for African American students differs based on whether or not their parents attended college.

A surprising finding in the current study was that no significant differences by generational status were found on the relationships with faculty scale. The research indicates that the social integration of first-generation and second-generation African American students may be influenced by the student's perceived institutional fit. In this context, institutional fit among African American students is determined through their interaction with both the campus environment and its institutional agents. The findings of the current study contradict previous research. Prior research found that first-generation students were less likely to develop relationships with faculty members and were less likely to perceive faculty as being concerned about their development (Pascarella & Terenzini, 1979; Posey, 2002; Whitmire, 1997). Cole (1999) found faculty interaction to be particularly important for first-generation African American students and discovered that their second-generation counterparts were less likely to interact, or establish personal relationships, with faculty.

Although it seems logical that college educated parents would be more likely to encourage their children to network with faculty, Cole (1999) hypothesized that faculty interaction could serve as a substitute for the academic guidance that second-generation students receive at home. It is also likely that a difference in faculty experiences was not found in the current study due to the first-year curriculum of colleges. Many first-year and introductory courses are taught by college staff or instructors who are particularly sensitive to the needs of first year students. It is likely that in the first college year both first and second-generation

67

African American students are receiving more faculty and staff attention than they can expect in subsequent years.

Generational Status & PCE Vocational & Practical Emphasis

A very interesting finding in this research was that no significant differences by generational status were reported on the practical and vocational emphasis scales. This contradicts prior studies which found first-generation students to be more career-oriented (Billson & Terry, 1982; Pascarella et al., 2003; Schuman, 2005; Slater, 1996) and more likely to take courses in the technical and vocational fields (Pascarella et al., 2003). Researchers have attributed the overrepresentation of first-generation students in the technical and vocational fields to weaker levels of academic preparation, and to the erroneous perception that humanities graduates do not earn much money (Schuman, 2005; Slater, 1996).

The findings of this study do not support the theory that first-generation students are more career-oriented. A possible reason why a difference was not found based on parents level of education may be that the students in this study had completed only one college semester. It is likely that the initial college courses focused on meeting basic college requirements and were not reflective of the students' academic or career aspirations. Another possible explanation may be found in the federal and state programs that support many first-generation students. Career counseling is a primary component in these programs and it is possible that the specially trained administrators they employ are more successful in illustrating to first-generation students the benefits of a liberal arts education. The research also reveals that first-generation students are more likely to be in remedial college courses where the focus is on basic cognitive skills like writing and math. It is likely that first-generation students recognize the long-term value of these courses.

Quality of Effort & College Grades

The current study found no significant correlations between students' expected grade point average and the thirteen quality of effort scales. In other words, there was no relationship discovered between the amount of effort that both first and second-generation students invested in activities linked to academic success and their expected grade point average. Given that library usage is positively associated with retention among African American students (Kuh &

Gonyea, 2004) it is interesting that a relationship between expected grade point average and quality of effort invested in the library was not found. There are some reasons why this relationship may not exist. Much of the literature on the college library argues against the perception of the library as just a place to study. The findings of this study suggested that first-year African American students are not equating their college library with academic success. Similar to the findings in the current research, Whitmire (2003) found that the grade point averages of minority students were not associated with the frequency of library usage. Although this seems counterintuitive, there may be several possible explanations. One explanation may be that since the first-year students in this study had only completed one college semester, they may have had inflated grade expectations. It is likely that the students in this study had not yet entered into the more challenging upper level courses. Another possible explanation may be that students are utilizing alternative resources, such as the internet. Perhaps students are logging into the library remotely. It is possible that first-year students do not equate these alterative methods of information gathering with library usage.

Conclusions

This research focused on student perceptions of the college environment and differences in student quality of effort as determined by parental level of education. While this research was unable to track a cohort of first and second-generation African American students throughout college, it contributes to the literature in the field by focusing on within group differences among African American students. Overall, this study found that:

- significant differences between first and second-generation African American students existed on seven of the PCE and QE correlation scales, the majority of which involved the library experiences scales.

- parental level of education affected students' perception of the college environment through their relationships with other students and in their experience of the college environment as emphasizing analytical and practical skills.

- generational status had no effect on the perception of the college's vocational and practical emphasis among African American students.

- no significant differences by generation status existed in the relationship between students' quality of effort and expected grade point average in the first year.

This research uncovered empirical evidence that the experiences of African American college students differ as a function of parental level of education and highlights the importance of recognizing the effects of within group differences and family background characteristics on the college experience of ethnic minority students. Differences were discovered between the perception of the college environment and the level of student involvement on the library experiences scale, indicating that parental level of education influences the manner by which African American students perceive and utilize the library and its resources. Researchers have acknowledged the library as an important tool for retention (Mallinckroft & Sedlacek, 1987; Whitmire, 1997), and this research confirms the central role of the academic library in the academic integration of first-generation African American students.

This study also found quantitative evidence that first and second-generation African American students perceive their role in the academic and social realms of the college differently. Previous research has found race (Attinasi, 1989; Dennis et al., 2005; DeSousa & Kuh, 1996; Hurtado et al., 1998; Kraemer, 1997; Nora, 1987) and generational status (Billson & Terry, 1982; Dennis et al., 2005; Lohfink & Paulsen, 2005; Pascarella et al., 2004; Saunders & Serna, 2004), to be separate factors influencing the academic and social integration of college students. This study investigated the interaction of race and generational status and found that parental level of education is a cause of within group differences among African American college students.

The current study did not find evidence of differences in the perception of the college's practical and vocational emphasis, despite other research (Schuman, 2005; Slater, 1996) findings that both first-generation and African American students are more career oriented in their approach to college. So it appears that practical and vocational emphasis may be more of a concern with regard to race than generational status. Finally, the current study found that students' quality of effort did not influence their expected grade point average. This indicates that the students surveyed did not perceive the amount of effort they exerted into factors associated with academic success in college to be related to the grades they expected to earn.

Overall, this research supports both previous research on the importance of perception of the college environment on academic success, and Pace's (1984) findings that the quality of effort that students put forth affects their experience of college. As such, this research provides information on areas of intervention for African American students in the first year of college.

70

Policy Implications & Recommendations

The findings of the current study reveal that first-generation African American students did not perceive the college environment as positively as their second-generation peers, and that this may affect their academic and social integration into college. The importance of this research is in what it contributes to the existing literature on social capital, defined as the formation of bonds with peers and institutional agents (Bourdieu 1986; Gonzalez et al., 2003; Pascarella at al., 2004; Saunders & Serna, 2004; Stanton-Salazar, 1997). According to Bourdieu (1986), the measurement of social capital is in the amount of resources "ranked to possession of a durable network of more or less institutionalized relationships of mutual acquaintance and recognition, in other words, to membership in a group" (Bourdieu, 1986, p. 248). Bourdieu (1986) stated that the volume of social capital one has depends on the magnitude of the network of connections an individual can mobilize. Portes (1998) argued that these network connections, or social networks, are constructed through investment strategies aimed at institutionalizing group relations. The maintenance of these relationships allows individuals access to the resources possessed by the members of their network.

This study shows that in PWIs, first-generation African American students do not have access to the same level of network connections as second-generation African American students. This means that the accumulation of social capital for first-generation African American students is impeded at PWIs. Fortunately, there are a number of steps that colleges and universities can take to improve the institutional environment and positively influence the experience of first-generation African American students. This can be accomplished through directed initiatives to foster social capital among first-generation African American students on both the student and the institutional level.

Student Level

In this study, the impact of limited social capital is reflected in the significant difference found by generational status in students' perception of their relationships with other students and groups. Second-generation African American students reported greater comfort in their interactions with other students than did first-generation African American students. In educational settings, social capital occurs in the cultivation of relationships with administrators, faculty members or other students. Social capital in the form of peer support has been found to be important in the academic adjustment of first-generation college students (Astin, 1984;

71

Billson & Terry, 1982; Richardson & Skinner, 1992; Tinto, 1993) and previous research indicates that students perceive their peers as better able to provide the type of encouragement instrumental to college outcomes, such as forming study groups, sharing notes and providing advice about classes (Richardson & Skinner, 1992). These are the types of supportive activities that the families and friends of first-generation students do not appear to be able to provide (Dennis et al., 2005).

This current research indicates that the existing bonds and bridges that create networks for first-generation African American students are not sufficient. The lack of interaction with other students, groups and activities exacerbates the formation of social capital among first-generation African American students. The findings of this study have important policy implications that can impact the social capital of first-generation African American college students. Colleges and universities can utilize bridging and bonding social capital to assist first-generation African American students in becoming academically and socially acclimated to the college environment (Putnam, 2000). On the student level, the colleges can,

- create summer bridge or orientation sessions aimed at first-generation families. These sessions would address specific concerns of first-generation students and include topics such as navigating the institution, cultivating student relationships, and identifying and utilizing college resources. These sessions would include academic open house events where faculty would be available to speak to prospective students and their parents about majors and possible career paths.

- design early identification and intervention efforts to create a sense of community and camaraderie among first-generation African American students. This would include mentoring or leadership programs with academic and social components, such as study groups and social outings. These programs would be designed to encapsulate the factors leading to academic success for first-generation African American students.

- provide programming to foster discussions among first-generation students on the barriers they encounter hindering their integration into college. Program topics would include, "How to Balance Your Family & School Commitments", "How to Declare a Major to Your Parents", and "How to Manage Your Home & School Identities".

- train college advisers to specialize in the needs of first-generation students. This would include maintaining a staff resource library containing information and current research on first-generation and African American students.

Institutional Level

Tinto's model of college retention highlights the importance of academic and social integration for disadvantaged and minority students. According to the model, in order to be successful students must identify with the new norms of the college environment and establish a role within its structure. However, the research on social capital in education suggests that first-generation students do not have access to the same amount of physical, social and emotional resources as their second-generation peers (Billson & Terry, 1982; Saunders & Serna, 2004; Zalaquett, 1999). The findings of this research indicate that first-generation and minority students have different experiences of college than their counterparts, and that this affects their level of institutional integration (Dennis et al., 2005; DeSousa & Kuh, 1996; Hurtado et al., 1998; Kraemer, 1997).

In the context of this study, parental level of education is an aspect of the Bourdieuian concept of social capital, in that it represents the intergenerational transfer of viewpoints, resources and information on education (Bourdieu, 1977). In this research, the effects of social capital were displayed in the differences between the perception of the college environment and quality of effort reported among first and second-generation African American students in the first year of college. These differences will affect how both groups come to perceive their role in institutions of higher education. Colleges and universities can actively assist in the process of academic and social integration among first-generation African American students by increasing their access to social capital on an institutional level. This can be accomplished through

- discussions with incoming first-generation students by college staff on the academic and social benefits of living on-campus and becoming involved with the campus community.
- aggressive outreach efforts by the campus career center to provide programming and career counseling to first-generation African American students. This can be accomplished by having career center staff participate in summer orientations and invited as guest lecturers in first-year core courses.

- provisions for earmarked financial aid, especially scholarships and grants, aimed at lessening the financial hardship of first-generation students.

- creation of ample college supported work-study positions on campus and an institutional commitment to serve the neediest students first.

- support programs designed to involve the parents of first-generation students in the college experience of their children. These programs must include college personnel who are familiar with the issues facing first-generation families and would address issues unfamiliar to first-generation parents, like completing a Free Application for Federal Student Aid.

- continuous outreach to parents of first-generation students. Efforts must be made to educate parents on the expectations of the college on their children, and on the academic benefits of students living and working on campus. This can be done through monthly newsletters to update parents on what their children are going through, such as preparing for midterm examinations or registering for classes.

- scheduling targeted programs during the non-traditional hours that typically meet the time constraints of first-generation students.

- re-evaluation of the level of accessibility that first-generation students have to college faculty and staff.

- possible inclusion of flexible hours of operation and release time for the staff members who assist in non-traditional programming efforts.

Libraries

Spencer et al. (2004) found that first-generation status leads to differing patterns of social and human capital acquisition and help-seeking behaviors in college. Particularly, this research uncovered significant differences in students' experience of the library, a source from which students can obtain detailed assistance with their academic and career goals. This is especially important given that the library has been identified as the only campus facility associated with the retention of African American undergraduates (Kuh & Gonyea, 2004). This study found that first-generation students reported having more difficulty in locating and evaluating information. This supports research done by Kuh & Gonyea's (2004) who studied over 300,000 CSEQ responses and found that only fifty percent of students surveyed reported feeling confident in their ability to locate good sources of information, and that nearly the same percentage admitted to difficulty in judging the quality of the information uncovered. It is important for colleges to insure that all first-year students are equipped with the basic knowledge necessary to effectively utilize the library. Institutions can foster comfort with the campus library through

- active efforts to recruit and hire library staff that is knowledgeable about, and reflective of, the student populations that they serve.
- emphasizing library skills and familiarizing students with the campus library in the first-year.
- marketing libraries must be recognized and utilized as information hubs. To accomplish this staff must educate students on how to utilize library systems, such as library search engines and intra-library loans.
- integrating on-going programs designed to instruct students in proper library usage.
- college orientations, first-year mission and core courses, and residence hall programming must be inclusive of activities that incorporate the use of the library and its resources, including the reference librarian.
- inclusion of library staff as instructors and advisers for first-year students.
- diversity training for library staff on how issues of race, class and gender affect library usage.
- creating library environments that reflect the diverse communities they serve. This would include the physical features of the library, such as the art work featured in the building and the book displays marketed in the welcome area.

Utilizing bonding and bridging social capital to address educational inequity requires that institutions critically examine their current norms and policies. The systemic student and institution based changes suggested by this research would create opportunities to allow for the successful academic and social integration of first-generation African American students.

Limitations

Given the findings of this study, it is important to note that the data was culled from a national data set to obtain a nationally representative sample. The data in this research was extracted from four-year predominately white public and private institutions. Therefore, the findings cannot be generalized to either explain the collegiate experience of first and second-generation students in HBCUs, or to explain the college experiences of other minority groups. It must also be noted that it is possible that some of the students indicating that their parents have graduated from college may actually be third-generation students, if their grandparents had also attended college. Since the data collection method utilized respondents from four-year PWIs across the nation, differences may exist in students' perception by college or in the institutional methods of data collection.

A limitation that Tanka (2002) noted in regard to the use of the CSEQ is also relevant to this study. While the CSEQ looks at a student's level of involvement, it does not differentiate 'effort' in terms of cultural specificity. For example, the CSEQ does not show whether or not the impact of time spent with minority faculty or in minority student organizations differs from time spent with all faculty or in campus wide organizations. Likewise, this study is unable to identify the effects of generational status on relationships with minority students, student groups and faculty members.

Another limitation is inherent in the methodology undertaken. This research relies primary on the correlational relationships found between the dependent variable, generation status, and the independent variables of perception of the college environment, quality of student effort, and expected grade point average. Studies utilizing correlations are among the most widely used analytical procedures in the behavioral sciences (Hinkle et al., 1981) and are worthwhile as sources of hypotheses about causation (Games, 1990), but they are the weakest type of quantitative study. Correlations among generation status and perception of the college environment, quality of effort and grade point average indicate an association or relationship among the variables. However, these relationships are non-directional and do not necessarily indicate that scores on one variable are caused by scores on the other. A myriad of extraneous factors may be responsible for these relationships. As Hinkle et al. (1981) states, "Causality must be inferred only in the context of the specific variables being correlated" (p. 87). This research did not assign controls on potentially mitigating influences, such as ethnicity, gender, socioeconomic status or prior educational experiences. It is also likely that the data set utilized included some proportion of students who participated in pre-college or summer enrichment programs, which may have influenced their initial perceptions of college.

Caution must be used in examining correlations so that individual differences do not become the source of all interpretations (Games, 1990). As a quantitative study, this research lacks the potential richness of discussion that could have been generated between the groups studied, particularly regarding their library experiences. Further research should be undertaken to place the needs of first-generation African American students in the proper perspective.

Areas for Future Research

Critics of Tinto's model (1993) argue its applicability to the needs and concerns of minority and disadvantaged students (Rendon, 1993; Tierney, 1992), specifically in regards to the process of integration. This research shows that race and socioeconomic status, as defined by parental level of education, affects a students' experience of college. However, qualitative research, particularly utilizing focus groups and interviews, would provide more in-depth information on how each group perceives college and becomes academically and socially integrated into the institution. Likewise, a study linking quantitative data with focused group interviews would provide insight into how each group experiences college. For example, it would be useful to examine how students describe their library usage or to gain first-hand accounts of what motivates second-generation African American students to become involved with other students and student groups.

The library was discovered to be a significant factor in the experience of first-generation African American students. While research has examined the effects of library experiences on the retention of ethnic minority students (Mallinckrodt & Sedlacek, 1987; Pascarella et al., 2004; Shoge, 2003; Whitmire, 2003), additional research must be undertaken to examine the effects of library usage on the academic and social integration of first-generation minority students.

Additionally, researchers have pointed out differences in the experiences of African American males and females in college ("The Persisting Racial Gap in College Student Graduation Rates", 2004; Simms et al., 1993;). Given these findings, future research efforts should examine the effects of parental level of education on first and second-generation African American male and female students.

REFERENCES

Allen, W. (1992). The color of success: African American college student outcomes at predominately white and historically black colleges. *Harvard Educational Review, 62,* 26-44.

Anderson, J. D. (2002). Race in American higher education: Historical perspectives on current conditions. In W.A. Smith, P.G. Altbach, and K. Lomotey, K. (Eds.), *The racial crisis in American higher education: Continued challenges for the twenty-first century* (pp. 3-21). Albany, NY: State University of New York.

Anyon, J. (1997). *Ghetto schooling: A political economy of urban educational reform.* New York, NY: Teachers College.

Arum, R., & Beattie, I.R. (2000). *The structure of schooling: Readings in sociology of education.* Mountainview, CA: Mayfield.

Astin, A. (1984). Student involvement: A developmental theory for higher education. *Journal of College Student Personnel, 25,* 297-308.

Astin, A., & Osguero, L. (2004). The declining 'equity' of American higher education. *Review of Higher Education, 27(3),* 321-341.

Attinasi, L.C. (1989). Getting in: Mexican Americans' perceptions of university attendance and the implications for freshman year persistence. *Journal of Higher Education, 60(3),* 247-277.

Baker, T.L., & Velez, W. (1996). Access to and opportunity in postsecondary education in the united states: A review. *Sociology of Education, 69,* 82-101.

Billson, J.M., & Brooks-Terry, M. (1982). In search of the silken purse: Factors in attrition among first-generation students. *College and University,* 57-75.

Billson, J.M., & Brooks-Terry, M. (1988). Tracing the disadvantages of first-generation college students: An application of Sussman's option sequence model. In S. Steinmetz (Ed.), *Family and support systems across the life span* (pp. 121-134). New York, NY: Plenum.

Blau, P. M., & Duncan, O. D. (1967). *The American occupational structure.* New York, NY: The Free Press.

Bourdieu, P. (1973). Three forms of theoretical knowledge. *Social Science Information, 12,* 53-80.

Bourdieu, P. (1977). *Outline of a theory of practice.* New York, NY: Cambridge University.

Bourdieu, P. (1986). The forms of capital. In J.G. Richardson (Ed.), *Handbook of theory and research for the sociology of education* (pp. 240-258). New York, NY: Greenwood Press.

Brint, S., & Karabel, J. (1989). Community colleges and the American social order. In A. Arum and I.R. Beattie (Eds.), *The structure of schooling: Readings in sociology of education* (pp. 463-474). Mountainview, CA: Mayfield.

Business remains the preferred degree of African American college students, but black students are looking into other fields. (2003). *The Journal of Blacks in Higher Education, 27,* 36-38.

Carroll, L. *The annotated alice: the definitive edition.* W.W. Norton & Company. New York: NY

Carter, D. F. (1999). The impact of institutional choice and environments on African American and white students' degree expectations. *Research in Higher Education, 40(1),* 17-41.

Carter, D. F. (2001). *A dream deferred? examining the degree aspirations of African American and white college students.* New York, NY: RutLedgeFalmer.

Cavanagh, S. (2004, October 20). Students Ill-Prepared for College, ACT Warns. *Education Week, 24(8),* 5.

Chavous, T. M. (2000). The relationships among racial identity, perceived institutional fit, and organizational involvement for African American students at a predominately white university. *Journal of Black Psychology, 26,* 79-100.

Chavous, T. M. (2002). African American college students in predominately white institutions of higher education: Considerations of race and gender. *Perspectives,* 142-150.

Cheatham, H. E. (1990). Africentricity and career development of African Americans. *Career Development Quarterly, 38(4),* 334-346.

Christie, N. G., & Dinham, S.M. (1991). Institutional and external influences on social integration in the freshman year. *Journal of Higher Education 62(4),* 412-436.

Coakley, K. (2003). What do we know about the motivation of African American students? *Harvard Educational Review, 73(4),* 524-559.

Cole, D. (1999). *Faculty-student interactions of African American and white college students at predominately white institutions.* Unpublished doctoral dissertation, Indiana University, Bloomington.

Coleman, J. S. (1988). Social capital in the creation of human capital. *The American Journal of Sociology, 94,* 95-120.

Coleman, J.S., Campbell, E.Q., Hobson, C.F., McPartland, J., Mood, A.M., Weinfeld, R. & York, R. (1966) Equality of Educational Opportunity. Washington, D.C.: US Department of Education.

Coleman, J., & Hoffer, T. (2003). Schools, families and communities. In A. Arum & I. R. Beattie (Eds.), *The structure of schooling: Readings in the sociology of education* (pp. 69-77). New York, NY: McGraw-Hill Higher Education.

Conchas, G. (2001). Structuring success and failure: Understanding variability in latino school engagement. *Harvard Educational Review,71(3)*, 475-504.

DeCoster, D.A. (1989). Review of college students experiences questionnaire. In J.C. Conoley & J.J. Kramers (Eds.), *The tenth mental measurements yearbook* (pp. 197-199). Lincoln, NE: University of Nebraska, Buros Institute of Mental Health.

de Jager, K. (2002). Successful students: Does the library make a difference? *Performance Measurement and Metrics, 3(3)*, 140-144.

Dennis, J. M., Phinney, J.S., & Chuateco, L.I. (2005). The role of motivation, parental support & peer support in the academic success of ethnic minority first-generation college students. *Journal of College Student Development, 46 (3)*, 223-236.

DeSousa, D. J., & Kuh, G.D. (1996). Does institutional racial composition make a difference in what black students gain from college? *Journal of College Student Development, 37(3)*, 257-267.

Durkheim, E. (1951).Suicide. Glencoe: The Free Press.

Elkins, S., Braxton, J.M. & James, G. W. (2000). Tinto's separation stage and its influence on first-semester college student persistence. *Research in Higher Education 41(2)*, 251-268.

Education Resources Institute and Institute for Higher Education Policy (1997). Missed opportunities: A new look at disadvantaged college aspirants. Boston and Washington, DC: Author. (ERIC Document Reproduction Service No EP420 257).

Flowers, L. (2002). The impact of college racial composition on African American students' academic and social gains: Additional evidence. *Journal of College Student Development, 43,* 403-410.

Flowers, L. (2004). Examining the effects of student involvement on African American college student development. *Journal of College Student Development, 45*(6), 633-654.

Games, P.A. (1990). Correlation and causation: A logical snafu. *Journal of Experimental Education, 58 (3),* 239-246.

Gibbons, M.M. (2004). Prospective first-generation college students: Meeting their needs through social cognitive career theory. *Professional School Counseling,* 91-99.

Gonzalez, K., Stoner, C., & Jovel, J. E. (2003). Examining the role of social capital in access to college for latinas: Toward a college opportunity framework. *Journal of Hispanic Higher Education, 2(1),* 146-170.

Gonyea, R.M., & Kish, K.A., Muthiah, R.N. & Thomas, A.D. (2003). *College Student Experiences Questionnaire: Norms for the Fourth Edition.* Bloomington, IN: Indiana University Center for Postsecondary Research, Policy & Planning.

Gonyea, R. M. & Kuh (1996). Does institutional racial composition make a difference in what black students gain from college? *Journal of College Student Development, 37,* 257-267.

Haycock, K. (2001). Closing the achievement gap. *Educational Leadership, 58,* 6-11.

Heisserer, D. & Parette, P. (2002). Advising at-risk students in college & university settings. *College Student Journal, 36(1),* 69-84.

Helm, E. J., Sedlacek, W., & Prieto, D. (1998). Career advising issues for African American entering students. *Journal of the First-Year Experience and Students in Transition, 10 (2),* 77-87

Hinkle, D.E., Wiersman, W., & Jurs, S.G. (1981) *Applied Statistics for the Behavioral Sciences.* Chicago, IL: Rand McNally College Publishing Company.

Horn, L. & Nuñez, A.-M. (2000). Mapping the road to college: First-generation students' math track, planning strategies, and context of support. (NCES 2000-153). U.S. Department of Education, *National Center for Education Statistics.* Washington, DC: U.S. Government Printing Office.

Horvat, E. M. (2003). The interactive effects of race and class in educational research: Theoretical insights from the work of pierre bourdieu. *Penn GSE Perspectives in Urban Education, 2(1),* 1-18.

Hsiao, K. P. (1992). First-generation college students. *ERIC Clearinghouse for Junior Colleges.* ED 351079. Los Angeles, CA.

Hu, S., & Kuh, G. D. (2003). Maximizing what students get out of college: Testing a learning productivity model. *Journal of College Student Development, 44(2),* 185-203.

Hurtado, S., & Carter, D. F. (1997). Effects of college transition and perceptions of the campus racial climate on latino students' sense of belonging. *Sociology of Education, 70,* 324- 345. Hurtado, S., Inkelaskk, Briggs, C. & Rhee, B.S. (1997). Difference in college access and choice among racial/ethnic groups: Identifying continuing barriers. *Research in Higher Education, 38,* 43-75.

Hurtado, S., Milem, J.F., Clayton-Pedersen, A.R., & Allen, W.R. (1998). Enhancing campus climates for racial/ethnic diversity: Educational policy & practice. *The Review of Higher Education, 21(3),* 279-302.

Hurtado, S., Milem, J. F., Clayton-Pedersen, A. R., & Allen, W. R. (1999). Enacting diverse learning environments: Improving the climate for racial/ethnic diversity in higher education institutions, *ASHE-ERIC Higher Education Report* (Vol. 26). Washington, DC: The George Washington University, Graduate School of Education and Human Development.

Ibarra, R.A. (2005) A place to belong: The library as prototype for context diversity. Paper presented at the meeting of the Twelfth National Conference of the Association of College and Research Libraries, 3-23, Minneapolis, MN.

Inman, W. E. & Mayes, L. (1999). The importance of being first: Unique characteristics of first-generation community college students. *Community College Review, 26(4),* 3-18.

Irons, P.H. (2002). *Jim crow's children: The broken promise of the brown decision.* NY: Viking.

Ishitani, T. (2003). A longitudinal approach to assessing attrition behavior among first-generation students: Time-varying effects of pre-college characteristics. *Research in Higher Education, 44(4),* 433-449.

Ishitani, T., & DesJardins, S.L. (2002). A longitudinal investigation of dropout from college in the united states. *Journal of College Student Retention: Research, Theory & Practice, 4(4),* 173-201.

Jones-Quartey, T.S. (1993). The academic library's role in the effort to improve ethnic minority retention. *The Educational Forum, 57,* 277-282.

Joseph, L. K. (1995). Institutional persistence among first-generation students: A test of the tinto model. Unpublished doctoral dissertation. University of West Virginia, West Virginia.

Kaplan, M. (1980). *What is an educated person? The decades ahead.* New York: Praeger Press.

Karunanayake, D., & Nauta, M. (2004.). The relationship between race and students' identified career role models and perceived role model influence. *The Career Development Quarterly, 52,* 225-234.

Kelly, M. C. (1995). Undergraduate retention and academic libraries. *College and Research Libraries News, 56,* 757-759.

Kraemer, B. (1997). The academic and social integration of hispanic students into college. *The Review of Higher Education, 20,* 163-179.

Kuh, G.D., & Gonyea, R.M. (2003). The role of the academic library in promoting student engagement in learning. *College & Research Library, 64(4),* 256-282.

Kuh, G. D., & Gonyea, R.M. (2004). The role of the academic library in promoting student engagement in learning. A paper presented to the 11th National Conference of the Association of College and Research Libraries. Charlotte, NC. Retrieved 6/10/04. www.ala.org/ala/acrl/acrlevents/nationalconference/03authorindex.htm.

Kuh, G. D., Pace, C. R., & Vesper, N. (1997). The development of process indicators to estimate student gains associated with good practices in undergraduate education. *Research in Higher Education, 38(4),* 435-454.

Lang, M. (1988). The black student retention problem in higher education: Some introductory perspectives. In M. F. Lang & C.A. Ford (Eds.), *Black Student Retention in Higher Education* (pp. 3-11). Springfield, IL: C. Charles C. Thomas.

Lohfink, M.M., & Paulsen, M.B., (2005). Comparing the determinants of persistence for first-generation and continuing-generation students. *Journal of College Student Development, 36(4),* 409-428.

London, H.B. (1989). Breaking away: A study of first-generation college students and their families. *American Journal of Education, 97,* 144-170.

London, H. B. (1992). Transformations: Cultural challenges faced by first-generation students. *New Directions for Community Colleges, 20(4),* 5-11.

Mallinckrodt, B. & Sedlacek, W. (1987). Student retention & the use of campus facilities by race. *NASPA Journal, 24,* 28-32.

McConnell, P. J. (2000). What community colleges should do to assist first generation students. *Community College Review, 28(3),* 75-88.

McDonough, P. M. (1997). *Choosing colleges: How social class and schools structure opportunity.* Albany, NY: State University of New York.

McGreggor, L. N., Mayleben, M. A., Buzzanga, V. L., Davis, S. F., & Becker, A. H. (1991). Selected personality characteristics of first-generation college students. *College Student Journal, 25(2),* 231-234.

McKay, K., & Kuh, G. (1994). A comparison of student effort and educational gains of caucasion and African American students at predominately white colleges and universities. *Journal of College Student Development, 35,* 217-223.

Mercillo, R. (2002). The challenge of first generation college students. *Chronicle of Higher Education, 48,* B10-12.

Metz, G. (1995). College careers of disadvantaged students: Opportunity, contradiction & limitation in higher education. Unpublished doctoral dissertation, Rutgers University, New Brunswick.

Metz, G. (2004). Getting ahead & staying behind at college: Towards a structurationist analysis of transformation in higher education opportunity. Unpublished Manuscript.

Mickey, R. C. (1988). *Counseling, advising and mentoring as retention strategies for black students in higher education.* Springfield, Il: Charles C. Thomas Publishers.

Middleton, T. (1997). *First generation college students: Cognitive development, personal development and satisfaction with college.* Unpublished Doctoral Dissertation, University of Iowa, Iowa.

National Center for Education Statistics (1998). First-generation students: Undergraduates whose parents never enrolled in post-secondary education. Washington, DC: US Department of Education. (ERIC Document Reproduction Service No. ED 420 235).

Nettles, T. (1988). *Factors related to black and white students' college performance: Toward black undergraduate student equality in American higher education.* New York: Green Press.

Nettles, T.M.,& Perna, L.W. (1997). *The African American Education Data Book, Volume One: Higher & Adult Education.* Fairfax, V.A. Frederick D. Patterson Research Institute of the College Fund, UNCF.

Noel, L. (1991). Increasing student retention: New challenges and potential. In L. Noel, R. Levitz, D. Saluri et al. (Eds.), *Increasing student retention: Effective programs and practices for reducing the dropout rate.* San Francisco: Jossey-Bass.

Noguera, P. (2003). *City schools and the American dream.* New York: Teachers College Press.

Nora, A. (1987). Determinants of retention among chicano college students: A structural model. *Research in Higher Education, 26,* 31-59.

Nuñez, A.-M. & Cuccaro-Alammis, S. (1998). *First-generation students: Undergraduates whose parents never enrolled in postsecondary education* (NCES 98082). U.S. Department of Education, National Center for Education Statistics. Washington, DC: U.S. Government Printing Office.

Orbe, M. P. (2004). Negotiating multiple identities within multiple frames: An analysis of first-generation college students. *Communication Education, 53(2),* 131-149.

Orfield, G. (1996). The growth of segregation: African Americans, latinos and unequal education. In A. Arum and I.R. Beattie (Eds.), *The structure of schooling: Readings in sociology of education* (pp. 194-206). Mountainview, CA: Mayfield Publishing Company.

Orfield, G. & Yun, J.T. (1999). *Re-segregation in American schools.* The Civil Rights Project Harvard University.

Orozco, C.D. (1999). Factors contributing to the psychosocial adjustment of mexican American college students. Doctoral dissertation, Northern Arizona University, 1999). *Dissertation Abstracts, 59,* 4359.

Pace, C.R. (1979). *Measuring outcomes of college: Fifty years of findings and recommendations for the future.* San Francisco: Jossey Bass.

Pace, C. R. (1984). Historical perspectives on student outcomes: Assessment with Implications for the Future. *NASPA Journal, 22(2),*10-18.

Pace, R., & Kuh, G.D. (1998) College student experiences questionnaire (4th ed.). Bloomington: Indiana University Center for Post-secondary Research and Planning.

Padron, E. J. (1992). *The challenge of first-generation college students: A miami-dade perspective.* San Francisco, CA: Jossey-Bass Publisher.

Pascarella, E. T., Pierson, C.T., Wolniak, G.C. & Terenzini, P.T. (2004). First-generation college students: Additional evidence on college experiences and outcomes. *Journal of Higher Education, 75(3),* 249-284.

Pascarella, E. T., Smart, J., Ethington, C., & Nettles, M. (1987). The influence of college on self concept: A consideration of race and gender differences. *American Educational Research Journal, 24,* 49-77.

Pascarella, E. T., & Terenzini, P.T. (1979). Interaction effects in spady and tinto's conceptual models of college attrition. *Sociology of Education, 52(4),* 197-210.

Pascarella, E. T., & Terenzini, P.T. (1991). *How college affects students: Findings and insights from twenty years of research.* San Francisco, CA: Jossey-Bass Publishers.

Pascarella, E. T., & Terenzini, P.T. (2003). Studying college in the twenty-first century: Meeting new challenges. *The Review of Higher Education, 21 (2),* 151-165.

Pascarella, E. T., Wolniak, G.C., Pierson, C.T., & Terenzini, P.T. (2003). Experiences and outcomes of first-generation students in community colleges. *Journal of College Student Development, 44(3),* 420-429.

Perna, L. W. (2000). Differences in the decision to attend college among African Americans, hispanics and whites. *The Journal of Higher Education, 71(2),* 117-141.

The persisting racial gap in college student graduation rates. (2004). Retrieved November 2, 2004 from http://www.jbhe.com/features/45_student_grad_rates.html.

Pike, G.R. (1999). The constant error of the halo in educational outcomes research. *Research in Higher Education, 40,* 61-86.

Pike, G.R., & Kuh, G. D. (2005) First and second-generation college students: A comparison of their engagement and intellectual development. *Journal of Higher Education, 76 (3)*, 276-300.

Portes, A. (1998). Social capital: Its origins and applications in modern sociology. *Annual Review of Sociology, 24*, 1-24.

Posey, S., & Cole, D. (2002). *What's going on? faculty-student interactions of black students attending predominately white institutions of higher learning*. Milwaukee, Wisconsin: University of Wisconsin.

Pratt, P.A., & Skagg, C.T. (1989). First-generation college students: Are they at greater risk for attrition than their peers? *Research in Rural Education, 6(2)* 31-34.

Putnam, R. (1995). Bowling alone: America's declining social capital. *Journal of Democracy 6.1*, 65-78.

Putnam, R. (2000). *Bowling alone: The collapse and revival of American community*. New York, NY: Simon & Schuster.

Reihl, R.J. (1994). The academic preparation, aspirations, and first-year performance of first-generation students. *College & University, 70(1)*, 14-19.

Rendon, R. (1995). *Facilitating retention and transfer for the first generation students in community colleges*. Paper presented at the New Mexico Institute, Rural Community College Initiate, Expanda, NM. (ERIC Document Reproduction Service No. ED383367)

Rippa, S.A. (1984). *Education in a Free Society: An American History* (5th ed.). New York, NY: McKay

Richardson, R. C., & Skinner, E.F. (1992). *Helping first-generation minority students achieve degrees*. San Francisco, CA: Jossey-Bass.

Roscigno, V. J., & Ainsworth-Darnell, J.W. (1996). Race, cultural capital and educational resources: Persistent inequalities and achievement returns. *Sociology of Education, 72(3)*, 22-34.

Saunders, M., & Serna, I. (2004). Making college happen: The college experiences of first-generation latino students. *Journal of Hispanic Higher Education, 3(2)*, 146-163.

Schilling, K., & Schilling, K. L. (1999). Increasing expectations for student effort. *About Campus*, 4-10.

Schuman, J. (2005, August 10). Students whose parents did not attend college under perform as undergraduates, study finds. *The Chronicle of Higher Education*.

Sewell, W. H. & Haller, A.O. & Portes, A. (1969). The educational and early occupational attainment process. *American Sociological Review, 34*, 82-92.

Shoge, R. C. (2003). The library as place in the lives of African Americans. Paper presented at the meeting of the Association of College and Research Libraries Eleventh National Conference, Chestertown, MD.

Simms, K.B., Knight, Jr., D.M., & Dawes, K.I. (1993). Institutional factors that influence the academic success of African American men. *Journal of Men's Studies, 1(3)*, 253-264.

Slater, R. B. (1996). The college course majors offering blacks the best financial rewards. *Journal of Blacks in Higher Education,12*, 84-87.

Somers, P., Woodhouse, S., & Cofer, J. (2000). *Persistence of first-generation college students.* Paper presented at the annual conference of the Association for the Study of Higher Education, Sacramento, CA.

Somers, P., Woodhouse, S. & Cofer, J. (2004). Pushing the boulder uphill: The persistence of first-generation college students. *NASPA Journal 41(3)*, 418-435.

Spady, W. G. (1970). Dropouts from higher education: An interdisciplinary review and synthesis. *Interchange, 1,* 64-85.

Spencer, K. L., Buchmann, C., & Landerman, L.R. (2004). Black and white achievement gap in the first college year: Evidence from a new longitudinal case study. In D. Bills and A. Portes (Eds.), *Research in Social Stratification and Mobility,* pp. 187-216. New York, NY: Elsevier.

Stage, F.K. & Hossler, D. (1989). Difference in family influences on college attendance plans for male and female ninth graders. *Research in Higher Education, 30*, 301-315.

Stamps, D. B. (1988). *Coping ability as a predictor of academic achievement among selected black college students: a case study.* Springfield, IL: C. Thomas Publishers.

Stanton-Salazar, R. (1997). A social capital framework for understanding the socialization of racial minority children and youths. *Harvard Educational Review,67,* 1-40.

Steele, C. M. (1997). A threat in the air: How stereotypes shape intellectual identity and performance. *American Psychologist, 52,* 613-629.

Steele, C. M. (1999). Thin ice: Stereotype threat and black college students. *The Atlantic Monthly,* 44-54.

Steelman, L. C. & Powell, B. (1989). Acquiring capital for college: The constraints of family configuration. *American Sociological Review, 54(5),* 844-855.

Swigart,T. E., & Murrell, P.H. (2001). Factors influencing estimates of gains made among African American and caucasian community college students. *Community College Journal of Research & Practice, 25,* 297-312.

Tanka, G. (2002). Higher education's self-reflexive turn: Toward an intercultural theory of student development. *Journal of Higher Education, 73(2),263-296.*

Terenzini, P.T., Rendon, L.I., Upcraft, M.L., Millar, S.B., Allison, K.W., Gregg, P.L. & Jalomo, R. (1994). The transition to college: Diverse students, diverse stories. *Research in Higher Education, 35 (1),* 57-73.

Terenzini, P.T., Springer, L., Pascarella, E.T. & Nora, A. (1995). Influences affecting the development of students' critical thinking skills. *Research in Higher Education, 36,* 23-39.

Terenzini, P. T., Springer, L., Yeager, P.M., Pascarella, E.T. & Nora, A. (1996). First-generation college students: Characteristics, experiences & cognitive development. *Research in Higher Education, 37(1),* 1-22.

Tierney, W. G. (1992). An anthropological analysis of student participation in college. *Journal of Higher Education, 63,* 604-618.

Ting, S.R. (1998). Predicting first-year grades and academic progress of college students of first-generation and low-income families. *Journal of College Admissions, 158,* 14-23.

Tinto, V. (1993). *Leaving college: rethinking the causes and cures of student attrition.* Chicago, IL: The University of Chicago.

Toppo, G. (2004, August 31). "Record number of minorities take the SAT." USA Today. Retrieved September 4, 2004, from http://www.usatoday.com/news/education/2004-08-31-sat-scores_x.htm

U.S. Department of Education, National Center for Education Statistics. (2002) *Digest of Educational Statistics, 2001.* (ACES 2000-130). Washington: D.C.: Thomas D. Snyder

Van Gennep, A. (1960) *The rites of passage.* Chicago, IL: University of Chicago.

Van T. Bui, K. (2002). First-generation college students at a four-year university: Background characteristics, reasons for pursuing higher education, and first-year experiences. *College Student Journal, 36(1),* 3-12.

Walker, K. L. and Satterwhite, T. (2002). Academic performance among African American and caucasian students: Is the family still important? *College Student Journal,* 113-129.

Warburton, E.C., Bugarin, R., and Nuñez, A.-M. (2001). Bridging the gap: Academic preparation and postsecondary success of first-generation students (NCES 2001-153). Washington: DC: National Center for Education Statistics. US Government Printing Office.

Weis, L. (1992). *Discordant voices in the urban community college.* San Francisco, CA: Jossey-Bass .

Wells, J. (1995). The influence of library usage on undergraduate academic success. *Australian Academic and Research Libraries, 26,* 121-128.

Whitmire, E. (1997). The campus environment for African American & white students: impact on academic library experiences. Paper presented at the meeting of the Association of College and Research Libraries 8th National Conference, Nashville, TN.

Whitmire, E. (1999). Racial differences in the academic library experiences of undergraduates. *Journal of Academic Librarianship, 25(1),* 33-37.

Whitmire, E. (2001). Factors influencing undergraduates' self-reported satisfaction with their information literacy skills. *Portal: Libraries and the Academy 1.4,* 409-420.

Whitmire, E. (2001b). A longitudinal study of undergraduates' academic library experiences. *The Journal of Academic Librarianship, 27(5),* 379-385.

Whitmire, E. (2003). Cultural diversity and undergraduates' academic library use. *Journal of Academic Librarianship, 29(3),* 148-161.

York-Anderson, D. C., & Bowman, S.L. (1991). Assessing the college knowledge of first generation and second generation college students. *Journal of College Student Development, 32,* 116-122.

Zalaquett, C. (1999). Do students of noncollege-educated parents achieve less academically than students of college educated parents? *Psychological Reports, 85,* 417-421.

APPENDIX

Correlations

Appendix A

Major Areas of Study for Study Participants

Major	Frequency	Percentage
Agriculture	11	1.0
Biological/Life Sciences	160	13.9
Business	195	16.9
Communications	86	7.5
Computer & Information Sciences	81	7.0
Education	89	7.7
Engineering	59	5.1
Ethnic, Cultural, Area Studies	19	1.6
Foreign Language & Literature	21	1.8
Health-Related	130	11.3
History	17	1.5
Undecided	93	8.1
Other	55	4.8
Humanities	53	4.6
Liberal/General Studies	7	0.6
Math	30	2.6
Multi-disciplinary Studies	13	1.1
Recreation/Sports Mngt	8	0.7
Physical Sciences	31	2.7
Pre-professional studies	163	14.4
Public Administration	19	1.6
Social Sciences	201	17.4
Visual & Performing Arts	48	4.2

Note. Students could select more than one major.

Appendix B

Intercorrelation of Quality of Effort (QE) & Perception of the College Environment Subscales among First-Generation Students

QE	Scholarship	Aesthetics	Analysis	Diversity	Info Literacy	Vocational Courses	Practical Courses
Library	0.06	0.09	0.04	0.04	0.11	0.04	0.05
Computer/Info.	0.01	0.03	0.08	-0.03	0.11	-0.01	0.03
Course Lrng.	0.31*	0.26*	0.23*	0.06	0.27*	0.10	0.19*
Writing Exp.	0.17*	0.19*	0.12	0.09	0.18*	0.11	0.14
Exp. w/ Faculty	0.10	0.17*	0.10	0.09	0.13*	0.15*	0.18*
Art/ Mus/The.	0.16*	0.19*	0.09	0.07	0.09	-0.00	0.08
Campus Facil.	0.09	0.10	0.05	0.03	0.08	0.07	0.11
Clubs	0.09	0.09	0.05	0.01	0.07	-0.01	0.06
Personal Exp.	0.11	0.12	0.09	0.08	0.18*	0.12	0.10
Student Acq.	0.19*	0.17*	0.17*	0.04	0.18*	0.11	0.08
Science/Quan.	0.04	0.10	0.09	0.10	0.06	0.12	0.12
Topics Conv.	0.23*	0.31*	0.23*	0.17*	0.22*	0.19*	0.15*
Info Conv.	0.26*	0.26*	0.28*	0.21*	0.24*	0.16*	0.12

*p<.01

QE	Rel. w/Stud.	Rel w/Admin	Rel w/Fac.
Library	0.07	0.17*	0.23*
Computer/Info.	0.07	0.05	0.14*
Course Lrng.	0.09	0.11	0.18*
Writing Exp.	0.10	0.10	0.13*
Exp. w/ Faculty	0.17*	0.19*	0.21*
Art/ Mus/The.	0.16*	0.16*	0.23*
Campus Facil.	0.23*	0.15*	0.15*
Clubs	0.15*	0.16*	0.18*
Personal Exp.	0.05	0.04	0.07
Student Acq.	0.19*	0.13*	0.13*
Science/Quan.	0.20*	0.15*	0.10
Topics Conv.	0.11	0.06	0.16*
Info Conv.	-0.01	0.01	0.08

Appendix C

Intercorrelations of Quality of Effort (QE) & Perception of the College Environment Scales among Second-Generation Students

QE	Scholarship	Aesthetics	Analysis	Diversity	Info Literacy	Vocational Courses
Library	0.15*	0.26*	0.25*	0.22*	0.16*	0.17*
Computer/IT	0.11*	0.19*	0.23*	0.16*	0.23*	0.11*
Course Lrng	0.18*	0.26*	0.25*	0.17*	0.18*	0.13*
Writing Exp.	0.10	0.18*	0.16*	0.17*	0.25*	0.15*
Exp. w/Fac.	0.14*	0.27*	0.25*	0.24*	0.16*	0.19*
Art/ Mus/The.	0.09	0.13*	0.11*	0.12*	-0.01	-0.01
Campus Fac.	0.18*	0.23*	0.21*	0.15*	0.16*	0.15*
Clubs	0.15*	0.14*	0.17*	0.05	0.05	0.08
Personal Exp.	0.00	0.16*	0.16*	0.15*	0.12*	0.11*
Student Acq.	0.20*	0.23*	0.22*	0.20*	0.12*	0.09
Science/Quant.	0.13*	0.17*	0.21*	0.15*	0.13*	0.14*
Topics Conv.	0.15*	0.24*	0.24*	0.17*	0.18*	0.16*
Info Conv.	0.15*	0.23*	0.24*	0.16*	0.10	0.11*

*p<.01

QE	Practical Courses	Rel. w/Stud.	Rel w/Admin	Rel w/Fac.
Library	0.25*	0.15*	0.25*	0.25*
Computer/IT	0.16*	0.09	0.13*	0.13*
Course Lrng	0.18*	0.10	0.14*	0.13*
Writing Exp.	0.17*	0.09	0.13*	0.07
Exp. w/Fac.	0.29*	0.19*	0.25*	0.24*
Art/ Mus/The.	0.09	0.08	0.07	0.10
Campus Fac.	0.23*	0.20*	0.18*	0.16*
Clubs	0.13*	0.12*	0.12*	0.15*
Personal Exp.	0.15*	0.09	0.09	0.09
Student Acq.	0.15*	0.21*	0.16*	0.16*
Science/Quan.	0.20*	0.06	0.08	0.05
Topics Conv.	0.21*	0.11*	0.14*	0.14*
Info Conv.	0.20*	0.15*	0.17*	0.16*

*p<.01

Wissenschaftlicher Buchverlag bietet

kostenfreie

Publikation

von

wissenschaftlichen Arbeiten

Diplomarbeiten, Magisterarbeiten, Master und Bachelor Theses
sowie Dissertationen, Habilitationen und wissenschaftliche Monographien

Sie verfügen über eine wissenschaftliche Abschlußarbeit zu aktuellen oder zeitlosen
Fragestellungen, die hohen inhaltlichen und formalen Ansprüchen genügt,
und haben **Interesse an einer honorarvergüteten Publikation**?

Dann senden Sie bitte erste Informationen über Ihre Arbeit per Email
an info@vdm-verlag.de. Unser Außenlektorat meldet sich umgehend bei Ihnen.

VDM Verlag Dr. Müller Aktiengesellschaft & Co. KG
Dudweiler Landstraße 125a
D - 66123 Saarbrücken

www.vdm-verlag.de

Druck:
Customized Business Services GmbH
im Auftrag der
KNV Zeitfracht GmbH
Ein Unternehmen der Zeitfracht - Gruppe
Ferdinand-Jühlke-Str. 7
99095 Erfurt